Vasco da Gama

and the Sea Route to India

Explorers of New Lands

Christopher Columbus
and the Discovery of the Americas

Hernándo Cortés
and the Fall of the Aztecs

Francis Drake
and the Oceans of the World

Francisco Coronado
and the Seven Cities of Gold

Ferdinand Magellan
and the Quest to Circle the Globe

Hernando de Soto
and His Expeditions Across the Americas

Francisco Pizarro
and the Conquest of the Inca

Marco Polo
and the Realm of Kublai Khan

Juan Ponce de León
and His Lands of Discovery

Vasco da Gama
and the Sea Route to India

Explorers of New Lands

Vasco da Gama
and the Sea Route to India

Rachel A. Koestler-Grack

Series Consulting Editor William H. Goetzmann
Jack S. Blanton, Sr. Chair in History and American Studies
University of Texas, Austin

CHELSEA HOUSE
PUBLISHERS
A Haights Cross Communications Company ®
Philadelphia

CHELSEA HOUSE PUBLISHERS
VP, NEW PRODUCT DEVELOPMENT Sally Cheney
DIRECTOR OF PRODUCTION Kim Shinners
CREATIVE MANAGER Takeshi Takahashi
MANUFACTURING MANAGER Diann Grasse

Staff for VASCO DA GAMA
EXECUTIVE EDITOR Lee Marcott
EDITORIAL ASSISTANT Carla Greenberg
PRODUCTION EDITOR Noelle Nardone
PHOTO EDITOR Sarah Bloom
COVER AND INTERIOR DESIGNER Keith Trego
LAYOUT 21st Century Publishing and Communications, Inc.

A Haights Cross Communications Company ®

www.chelseahouse.com

First Printing

9 8 7 6 5 4 3 2 1

Library of Congress Cataloging-in-Publication Data

Koestler-Grack, Rachel A., 1973–
    Vasco da Gama and the sea route to India/Rachel A. Koestler-Grack
       p. cm.–(Explorers of new lands)
    Includes bibliographical references and index.
    ISBN 0-7910-8611-9 (hardcover)
  1. Gama, Vasco da, 1468–1524–Juvenile literature. 2. Gama, Vasco da, 1469–1524–
Travel–India–Juvenile literature. 3. Explorers–Portugal–Biography. 4. Discoveries in
geography–Portuguese. I. Title. II. series.
G286.G2K64 2005
910'.92–dc22

                                                              2005007702

All links and web addresses were checked and verified to be correct at the time of publication.
Because of the dynamic nature of the web, some addresses and links may have changed since
publication and may no longer be valid.

Table of Contents

Introduction

by William H. Goetzmann
Jack S. Blanton, Sr. Chair in History and American Studies
University of Texas, Austin

Explorers have always been adventurers. They were, and still are, people of vision and most of all, people of curiosity. The English poet Rudyard Kipling once described the psychology behind the explorer's curiosity:

"Something hidden. Go and find it. Go and
    look behind the Ranges—
Something lost behind the Ranges. Lost and
    waiting for you. Go!" [1]

Miguel de Cervantes, the heroic author of *Don
Quixote*, longed to be an explorer-conquistador. So
he wrote a personal letter to King Phillip II of
Spain asking to be appointed to lead an expedition
to the New World. Phillip II turned down his
request. Later, while in prison, Cervantes gained
revenge. He wrote the immortal story of *Don
Quixote*, a broken-down, half-crazy "Knight of La
Mancha" who "explored" Spain with his faithful
sidekick, Sancho Panza. His was perhaps the first
of a long line of revenge novels—a lampoon of the
real explorer-conquistadors.

Most of these explorer-conquistadors, such as
Columbus and Cortés, are often regarded as heroes
who discovered new worlds and empires. They
were courageous, brave and clever, but most of
them were also cruel to the native peoples they
met. For example, Cortés, with a small band of
500 Spanish conquistadors, wiped out the vast

Aztec Empire. He insulted the Aztecs' gods and tore down their temples. A bit later, far down in South America, Francisco Pizarro and Hernando de Soto did the same to the Inca Empire, which was hidden behind a vast upland desert among Peru's towering mountains. Both tasks seem to be impossible, but these conquistadors not only overcame nature and savage armies, they stole their gold and became rich nobles. More astounding, they converted whole countries and even a continent to Spanish Catholicism. Cathedrals replaced blood-soaked temples, and the people of South and Central America, north to the Mexican border, soon spoke only two languages—Portuguese in Brazil and Spanish in the rest of the countries, even extending through the Southwest United States.

Most of the cathedral building and language changing has been attributed to the vast numbers of Spanish and Portuguese missionaries, but trade with and even enslavement of the natives must have played a great part. Also playing an important part were great missions that were half churches and half farming and ranching communities. They offered protection from enemies and a life of stability for the natives. Clearly vast numbers of natives took to these missions. The missions vied with the cruel native caciques, or rulers, for protection and for a constant food supply. We have to ask ourselves: Did the Spanish conquests raise the natives' standard of living? And did a religion of love appeal more to the natives than ones of sheer terror, where hearts were torn out and bodies were tossed down steep temple stairways as sacrifices that were probably eaten by dogs or other wild beasts? These questions are something to think about as you read the Explorers of New Lands series. They are profound questions even today.

"New Lands" does not only refer to the Western Hemisphere and the Spanish/Portuguese conquests there. Our series should probably begin with the fierce Vikings—Eric the Red, who discovered Greenland in 982, and Leif Ericson, who discovered North America in 1002, followed, probably a year later, by a settler named Bjorni. The Viking sagas (or tales passed down through generations) tell the stories of these men and of Fredis, the first woman discoverer of a New Land. She became a savior of the Viking men when, wielding a broadsword and screaming like a madwoman, she single-handedly routed the native Beothuks who were about to wipe out the earliest Viking settlement in North America that can be identified. The Vikings did not, however, last as long in North America as they did in Greenland and Northern England. The natives of the north were far tougher than the natives of the south and the Caribbean.

Far away, on virtually the other side of the world, traders were making their way east toward China. Persians and Arabs as well as Mongols established a trade route to the Far East via such fabled cities as Samarkand, Bukhara, and Kashgar and across the Hindu Kush and Pamir Mountains to Tibet and beyond. One of our volumes tells the story of Marco Polo, who crossed from Byzantium (later Constantinople) overland along the Silk Road to China and the court of Kublai Khan, the Mongol emperor. This was a crossing over wild deserts and towering mountains, as long as Columbus's Atlantic crossing to the Caribbean. His journey came under less dangerous (no pirates yet) and more comfortable conditions than that of the Polos, Nicolo and Maffeo, who from 1260 to 1269 made their way across these endless wastes while making friends, not enemies, of the fierce Mongols. In 1271, they took along Marco Polo (who was Nicolo's son and Maffeo's nephew). Marco became a great favorite of Kublai Khan and stayed in China till 1292. He even became the ruler of one of Kublai Khan's largest cities, Hangchow.

Before he returned, Marco Polo had learned of many of the Chinese ports, and because of Chinese trade to the west across the Indian Ocean, he knew of East Africa as far as Zanzibar. He also knew of the Spice Islands and Japan. When he returned to his home city of Venice he brought enviable new knowledge with him, about gunpowder, paper and paper money, coal, tea making, and the role of worms that create silk! While captured by Genoese forces, he dictated an account of his amazing adventures, which included vast amounts of new information, not only about China, but about the geography of nearly half of the globe. This is one hallmark of great explorers. How much did they contribute to the world's body of knowledge? These earlier inquisitive explorers were important members of a culture of science that stemmed from world trade and genuine curiosity. For the Polos crossing over deserts, mountains and very dangerous tribal-dominated countries or regions, theirs was a hard-won knowledge. As you read about Marco Polo's travels, try and count the many new things and descriptions he brought to Mediterranean countries.

Besides the Polos, however, there were many Islamic traders who traveled to China, like Ibn Battuta, who came from Morocco in Northwest Africa. An Italian Jewish rabbi-trader, Jacob d'Ancona, made his way via India in 1270 to the great Chinese trading port of Zaitun, where he spent much of his time. Both of these explorer-travelers left extensive reports of their expeditions, which rivaled those of the Polos but were less known, as are the neglected accounts of Roman Catholic friars who entered China, one of whom became bishop of Zaitun.[2]

In 1453, the Turkish Empire cut off the Silk Road to Asia. But Turkey was thwarted when, in 1497 and 1498, the Portuguese captain Vasco da Gama sailed from Lisbon around the tip of Africa, up to Arab-controlled Mozambique, and across the

Indian Ocean to Calicut on the western coast of India. He faced the hostility of Arab traders who virtually dominated Calicut. He took care of this problem on a second voyage in 1502 with 20 ships to safeguard the interests of colonists brought to India by another Portuguese captain, Pedro Álvares Cabral. Da Gama laid siege to Calicut and destroyed a fleet of 29 warships. He secured Calicut for the Portuguese settlers and opened a spice route to the islands of the Indies that made Portugal and Spain rich. Spices were valued nearly as much as gold since without refrigeration, foods would spoil. The spices disguised this, and also made the food taste good. Virtually every culture in the world has some kind of stew. Almost all of them depend on spices. Can you name some spices that come from the faraway Spice Islands?

Of course most Americans have heard of Christopher Columbus, who in 1492 sailed west across the Atlantic for the Indies and China. Instead, on four voyages, he reached Hispaniola (now Haiti and the Dominican Republic), Cuba and Jamaica. He created a vision of a New World, populated by what he misleadingly called Indians.

Conquistadors like the Italian sailing for Portugal, Amerigo Vespucci, followed Columbus and in 1502 reached South America at what is now Brazil. His landing there explains Brazil's Portuguese language origins as well as how America got its name on Renaissance charts drawn on vellum or dried sheepskin.

Meanwhile, the English heard of a Portuguese discovery of marvelous fishing grounds off Labrador (discovered by the Vikings and rediscovered by a mysterious freelance Portuguese sailor named the "Labrador"). They sent John Cabot in 1497 to locate these fishing grounds. He found them, and Newfoundland and Labrador as well. It marked the British discovery of North America.

In this first series there are strange tales of other explorers of new lands—Juan Ponce de León, who sought riches and possibly a fountain of youth (everlasting life) and died in Florida; Francisco Coronado, whose men discovered the Grand Canyon and at Zuñi established what became the heart of the Spanish Southwest before the creation of Santa Fe; and de Soto, who after helping to conquer the Incas, boldly ravaged what is now the

American South and Southeast. He also found that the Indian Mound Builder cultures, centered in Cahokia across the Mississippi from present-day St. Louis, had no gold and did not welcome him. Garcilaso de la Vega, the last Inca, lived to write de Soto's story, called *The Florida of the Inca*—a revenge story to match that of Cervantes, who like Garcilaso de la Vega ended up in the tiny Spanish town of Burgos. The two writers never met. Why was this—especially since Cervantes was the tax collector? Perhaps this was when he was in prison writing *Don Quixote.*

In 1513 Vasco Núñez de Balboa discovered the Pacific Ocean "from a peak in Darien"[3] and was soon beheaded by a rival conquistador. But perhaps the greatest Pacific feat was Ferdinand Magellan's voyage around the world from 1519 to 1522, which he did not survive.

Magellan was a Portuguese who sailed for Spain down the Atlantic and through the Strait of Magellan—a narrow passage to the Pacific. He journeyed across that ocean to the Philippines, where he was killed in a fight with the natives. As a recent biography put it, he had "sailed over the edge of the world."[4] His men continued west, and the *Victoria,* the last of his five ships, worn and battered, reached Spain.

Sir Francis Drake, a privateer and lifelong enemy of Spain, sailed for Queen Elizabeth of England on a secret mission in 1577 to find a passage across the Americas for England. Though he sailed, as he put it, "along the backside of Nueva Espanola"[5] as far north as Alaska perhaps, he found no such passage. He then sailed west around the world to England. He survived to help defeat the huge Spanish Armada sent by Phillip II to take England in 1588. Alas he could not give up his bad habit of privateering, and died of dysentery off Porto Bello, Panama. Drake did not find what he was looking for "beyond the ranges," but it wasn't his curiosity that killed him. He may have been the greatest explorer of them all!

While reading our series of great explorers, think about the many questions that arise in your reading, which I hope inspires you to great deeds.

Notes

1. Rudyard Kipling, "The Explorer" (1898). See Jon Heurtl, *Rudyard Kipling: Selected Poems* (New York: Barnes & Noble Books, 2004), 7.

2. Jacob D'Ancona, David Shelbourne, translator, *The City of Light: The Hidden Journal of the Man Who Entered China Four Years Before Marco Polo* (New York: Citadel Press, 1997).

3. John Keats, "On First Looking Into Chapman's Homer."

4. Laurence Bergreen, *Over the Edge of the World: Magellan's Terrifying Circumnavigation of the Globe* (New York: William Morrow & Company, 2003).

5. See Richard Hakluyt, *Principal Navigations, Voyages, Traffiques and Discoveries of the English Nation*, section on Sir Francis Drake.

Conquering
the Impossible

The sailors were beginning to tire of the smell of salt-water. Its burning vapors hung in the humid air. And although they had left the African coast 26 days before, their nostrils were still raw. Traveling by ship in 1498 held no luxuries for a seaman. The drinking water was often rancid, and the food was spoiled or stale. A sailor's sleeping quarters were thick with body odor and crowded with sick shipmates. So why would a man choose such a weary career?

The crew of Vasco da Gama's expedition did not need much time to answer that question. The horror of ocean tempests was calmed by the adventure of visiting new lands. Rotten ship food was alternated with the exotic fruits, vegetables, and meats that the sailors had never before tasted. The risk of death was worth a chance at conquering the impossible.

On May 20, 1498, da Gama and his crew had done just that—the impossible. The lookout, Ahmad, spotted high land. He identified the spot as Kotta Point. Vasco da Gama stood on the prow (the front deck of the ship) peering out over the blue waters of South India. Ahmad walked up to the commander. "We have arrived," he announced. "We are just north of Calicut! Here is the land where you desired to go."[1]

Before their eyes was the city of Calicut, India. A place of tales, where gold, silk, valuable spices, and precious gems were piled high at every corner.

After nearly 11 months, the long journey from Portugal to India was over. Thousands of weary miles of ocean travel were behind them. Many of the crewmen's companions had perished on the way, victims of scurvy, infection, or fever. Their bodies lay deep in the waters of the Atlantic and Indian Oceans. The survivors had endured terrifying stormy waters and hostile encounters with the natives. The hard sea voyage had put the crew within reach of the golden lands of the East. What was once a grand dream was now a grander reality. The sea road to the Indies had been discovered, charted by the ruthless commander Vasco da Gama. But the adventure was far from over.

On that first morning after da Gama's expedition arrived, he sent one of his men who spoke Arabic and Hebrew onto the shore. The natives took the sailor to the home of two Arabs who spoke his language. The Arabs asked what had brought the fleet to India. The sailor replied that da Gama and his men were seeking Christians and spices.

Da Gama's arrival in Calicut did not represent the first contact between the peoples of Europe and India, but da Gama's expedition did represent a true opening up of the East.

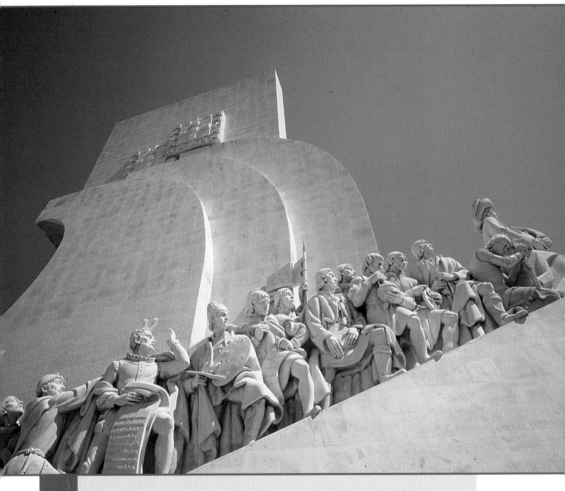

The "Monument to the Discoveries" is a leading attraction in Belem, Portugal, where the Tagus River meets the Atlantic Ocean. The monument commemorates the Portuguese Age of Discovery.

Da Gama would return to his homeland, Portugal. His discovery catapulted the nation into being a world power in trade. But his ruthless temper and callous cruelty also created many enemies across the oceans. His actions became a constant nuisance to Portuguese merchants, who were on steady lookout for Arab attackers. Nevertheless, Vasco da Gama was one of the greatest men of his era. His courage and determination opened the door for exploration and inspired other sailors to set out in search of new lands.

Test Your Knowledge

1 Which of the following best describes conditions for sailors in 1498?

   a. Fresh drinking water and food were always in abundance.

   b. Sleeping quarters were kept clean and disease-free.

   c. Water and food were often rancid, and quarters were filled with body odor.

   d. Weather and navigation were never a problem.

2 What made the seaman's life worthwhile?

   a. The idea of adventure

   b. Exotic meats and fruits from new lands

   c. The glory of cheating death

   d. All of the above

3 How long was the sea voyage from Portugal to India?

   a. One year

   b. Eleven months

   c. Six months

   d. Less than six months

4 What was da Gama seeking in India?

   a. Christians and spices

   b. Silver and gold

   c. A military advantage over the Spanish

   d. Rare herbs and medicines

What was the result of da Gama's discovery?

a. The understanding that the world was round

b. Riches in gold and silver for the king of Portugal

c. The elevation of Portugal to a world trading power

d. None of the above

ANSWERS: 1. c; 2. d; 3. b; 4. a; 5. c

A Brave Seaman

On the coast of Portugal, 60 miles south of Lisbon, lies the small seaside town of Sines. The sandy shoreline rises into rocky cliffs. Thick green undergrowth crawls up the slopes, dotted with the bright yellow flowers of the *tojo*, an evergreen shrub that grows brilliant in Sines but is seldom found elsewhere in the world. Here in this quiet fishing village stood a small humble house. Though the owner was considered a nobleman, the house was neither large nor elegant. At this house in the 1460s, Vasco da Gama was born. (The exact date of his birth is in question. Most historians believe he was born between 1460 and 1469.) Vasco's father was Estevão da Gama, a worthy seaman and an officer to the Portuguese crown. His mother was Izabel Sodré. Her family was of English descent. "Sodré" was actually a Portuguese mispronunciation of the English name "Sudley." Little did Izabel know that the small child she cradled in her arms was destined for great adventure. Vasco had two older brothers, Paulo and Ayres. He also had one sister, Thereza.

Sandy soil made farming difficult in Sines. For hundreds and perhaps even thousands of years, the villagers made their living as fishermen. Born on the seacoast, Vasco learned the life of a seaman at an early age. He quickly became a strong swimmer. His father and older brothers taught him how to row, steer a boat, and handle a sail. He learned the proper way to haul in heavy fishing nets filled with their silvery catch. Vasco found sea life adventurous.

A statue of Vasco da Gama sits in front of a church in the port town of Sines, Portugal, where da Gama was born. Since no formal education was available in Sines, da Gama went to Évora for schooling.

He often gazed at the far-off horizon, watching ships sail south to the Mediterranean ports or Morocco, or even to the exotic coast and islands of West Africa. At times, Vasco and his brothers gathered around the sailors as they worked. They listened to the men tell fantastic tales of the ocean. The wide-eyed boys heard stories about wicked storms and shipwrecks, wild sea creatures, and mysterious landings on unknown shores.

No formal education was available in the simple fishing town of Sines. When Vasco was ready for school, he traveled to Évora, a bustling town in the hills about 70 miles northeast of Sines. This strange city seemed like a foreign country to Vasco. The rich vegetation, which stretched for miles in every direction, surprised him. There were orchards, vineyards, and groves of olive, cork, and chestnut trees. Fertile farms and fields of rye dotted the landscape. The land was far different from the rocky shores and sandy patches that made up his hometown.

Once in the city, Vasco marveled at the narrow cobblestone streets and tall stone buildings. While walking, he came upon the grand palace of the Portuguese king. He gazed with awe at the many guardsmen with their shiny helmets standing in front of the gates. More guards paced back and forth high up on the wall. Little did the boy know that one day he would spend much time inside those massive walls with the king. The serious guardsmen who now looked past this young lad would later bow before him.

It took Vasco some time to get used to the different way of life in Évora. The people even looked different from the bronze-skinned, rough-faced townsfolk of Sines. They were fairer, taller, and thinner. In Évora, people dressed in clothes Vasco had never seen before. Many wore strange sheepskin coats, often with the wool turned to the outside. Men wore pants that were split up the inside of the leg and tied with laces. Each day, the women would come to the stone fountains and fill red clay jars with water. They then balanced the great vessels on their heads and gracefully walked home. Visitors from foreign countries often passed through the city. Vasco learned about many cultures and listened to new thoughts and ideas. Certainly at times, Vasco got homesick. He would climb the winding granite staircase of the cathedral tower. From high above the busy streets, he looked south to the green and blue horizon of his boyhood home.

Vasco's school years rolled by. He mastered his studies in navigation, mathematics, and astronomy. He grew into a striking and bold young man. Many of Vasco's friends thought he was daring and unruly. He got into trouble more than once. One night while walking the streets of nearby Setúbal, the night watch guard tried to stop Vasco. Vasco had the hood of his cloak over his head, covering his face. The watchman thought he looked suspicious. When the guard demanded his name, Vasco simply replied, "I am no criminal."[2] He boldly walked away.

SETTING OFF TO SEA

Around age 15, Vasco began working as a seaman. He put his education to practical use during voyages to West Africa, then called the Guinea Coast. His life at sea brought to mind all the tales he heard years ago on the docks of Sines. On his journeys, he learned how to navigate his ship skillfully through storms and rolling fog and along rocky coastlines. Before long, Vasco proved to be a strong and promising sailor. He mastered the basic skills of navigation: how to read the stars and the winds, the clouds and currents.

While Vasco was running trading ships back and forth from West Africa, new sea discoveries were

(continued on page 16)

Discovering the African Coast

In the history of exploration, 1415 marks an important breaking point. It was the start of the "Age of Discovery." In this year, Prince Henry of Portugal attacked the Moroccan city of Ceuta. Prince Henry, better known as Henry the Navigator, discovered a profitable trade business between Moroccan cities and the gold countries to the south. He desired to get his hands on West African trade.

At that time, Arab Muslims controlled trade in West Africa. So Henry formed an enterprise to explore the Moroccan coast and establish a Portuguese foothold there. But first, Henry had to find captains willing to embark on the journey. Portuguese sailors were afraid to explore the coast beyond Cape Bojador. They feared the sea was too shallow, the streams too narrow, and the land barren. They believed that if they sailed beyond the cape, they would never be able to return.

By 1433, Henry's captains discovered the Azores Islands, colonized the Madeira Islands, and claimed the Canary Islands. But they still had not passed Cape Bojador. Finally, Henry sent out Captain Gil Eannes and told him not to return unless he had successfully passed the cape. Apparently, Henry's

threats worked. In 1434, Captain Eannes passed
Cape Bojador, destroying any mental barrier that
stood between the captains and exploration.

After Eannes's voyage, Portuguese explorers
traveled bit by bit down the West African coast.
Captain Alfonso Baldaya reached Rio de Oro in
1436. Nuno Tristão passed Cape Blanco in 1441.
And in 1445, Dinis Dias traveled through Cape
Verde. When Henry died in 1460, his captains had
journeyed as far as Sierra Leone. From 1469 to
1474, the Portuguese explorer Fernão Gomes held
control of all West African trade. In return, he
promised to discover 600 kilometers of coastline a
year. During his time, the Portuguese explored the
coast down to just south of the equator.

In 1482, Diogo Cão discovered the Congo
River and sailed to Cape Santa Maria. During
his second voyage in 1485, he pushed even
farther south to present-day Namibia. In 1488,
Bartholomew Diaz led another expedition along
the African coast. During this voyage, a storm
accidentally blew him around the Cape of Good
Hope. Then, in 1497, Vasco da Gama used Diaz's
route to sail all the way to India.

(continued from page 13)

being made. In 1488, a Portuguese explorer named Bartholomew Diaz also traveled to the Guinea Coast with his three ships. During a fierce storm, the fleet was unexpectedly swept around the southern tip of Africa. No Portuguese ship had ever ventured into these waters. Diaz believed he had discovered a sea route to India. He wanted to try to sail onward. The terrifying experience of the storm soured his crew's attitude. They did not want to risk their lives on the violent, unknown seas. Instead, they mutinied against Diaz. Disappointed, he was forced to turn back.

Diaz reached Portugal at the end of 1488 and reported his discovery to King John II. This news excited the king. India was known for its great wealth. Now, these treasures were open to the ships of Portugal. For this reason, he named the peninsula off the South African coast the Cape of Good Hope. But King John had difficulty finding men who were willing to go on such a mission. Word got out about the stormy voyage of Diaz's crew. After Diaz's experience, many sailors were too frightened to sail around the Cape of Good Hope. Also, the Egyptian sultan and the rulers of powerful Venice became

Prince Henry the Navigator hoped to get a piece of the West African trade for Portugal in the fifteenth century. To do so, he began sending captains to explore the coast and establish a foothold there.

angered by the idea of Portugal trading with India. This area had always been their trading spot. King John feared that these countries might attack Portugal if he went ahead with the mission. Meanwhile in 1492, Christopher Columbus and the crews of his Spanish ships discovered the Americas. Spanish and Portuguese ships began traveling the Atlantic Ocean to the Caribbean Islands for trade. For these reasons, the king delayed the venture for 10 years.

Sometime during his early career, da Gama served on a sea mission for the Portuguese government. In 1492, King John sent him to Setúbal to seize French vessels in retaliation for raids against Portuguese shipping. He obviously impressed the officials. Dom Manuel, the duke of Beja and later King Manuel the Fortunate, found him a likely candidate for an important mission. King John needed a commander to lead a fleet of ships to chart a sea route to India. Dom Manuel believed da Gama was their man.

According to some historians, King John originally planned to send da Gama's father—Estevão da Gama—on the mission. Because Estevão had since died, the position fell to Vasco. Vasco's education and years at sea proved him a worthy seaman and a natural leader. In those days, ship crews were made up of tough, rowdy fellows, held in line only by strict discipline and respect for their captain. Like Diaz's, many voyages failed because of mutiny and overthrow on the high seas. Vasco da Gama was known by his men to be harsh but fair-minded. Not only would da Gama need to know how to manage his crew, he would also need skills in dealing with foreign cultures. His experience in Évora no doubt helped him develop a talent for communicating with foreigners.

In any case, da Gama's family had a reputation for bravery. Dom Manuel and his shrewd group of advisors found da Gama diplomatic, strong, and commanding. King John was in close contact with Dom Manuel. The king respected his recommendation and placed the key to India in da Gama's hand.

Dom Manuel allowed da Gama to take one of his brothers with him on the mission. Vasco chose Paulo, for whom he had a deep admiration. Before Paulo could accept, however, Vasco had to make an important plea on his brother's behalf. He needed to secure a royal pardon for Paulo. Years earlier, Paulo attacked and wounded a judge in Setúbal during a quarrel. At the time of the commission, Paulo was a fugitive outlaw. King John told Vasco, "For love of you, I pardon him my justice."[3] But the king added a condition. The pardon was only granted if Vasco and Paulo completed a successful mission to India. Vasco agreed and bowed his head to the king. He immediately began preparations for his historic voyage.

Test Your Knowledge

1 What is the *tojo*?
   a. A type of sailing ship
   b. A rare evergreen shrub
   c. A rare spice from India
   d. None of the above

2 Da Gama's hometown of Sines was known
   a. for its rich soil and farming.
   b. for its gold and spices.
   c. as a modest fishing village.
   d. for all of the above.

3 What did the young da Gama study in Évora?
   a. English, French, and Italian
   b. Navigation, mathematics, and astronomy
   c. Greek and Latin
   d. Swordsmanship and archery

4 What did Bartholomew Diaz discover?
   a. A likely sea route from Europe to India
   b. The continent of Africa
   c. The Ganges River in India
   d. None of the above

5 Why did King John delay in opening trade
routes between Portugal and India?

   a. Many sailors were afraid to sail around the
      Cape of Good Hope.

   b. The rulers of Egypt and Venice resented the
      idea of Portugal trading with India.

   c. Columbus's discovery of the Americas opened
      Portuguese trade routes to the Caribbean.

   d. All of the above.

ANSWERS: 1. b; 2. c; 3. b; 4. a; 5. d

Sailing
the Fleet

Vasco da Gama had much to prepare for the sailing of this hazardous journey. According to Diaz, navigating the churning waters off the Cape of Good Hope was difficult and dangerous. Da Gama decided that a new type of ship, called the caravel, might make crossing these restless waters easier. In the past, ship decks were deeply curved. Too much boat above the water line caused the vessels to dip and sway. Da Gama ordered low-built ships with level decks and wide hulls. He hoped these flat-bottomed boats would be more stable than earlier ships.

Carpenters prepared three ships for the trip. Da Gama chose the *São Gabriel* as his flagship and appointed Gonçalo Álvares as its captain. Álvares was a competent mariner who later achieved the important position of pilot-major of India. Pero D'Alenquer, who accompanied Diaz on the cape voyage, became the flagship pilot. The pilot was the most important person on the ship. Typically, a captain received his position because of family name or social status, or as a reward for some great deed, rather than for his reputation as a skilled seaman. A pilot bore the heaviest responsibility of navigation. In D'Alenquer's case, this responsibility was tripled, as he would lead the entire fleet. Da Gama's confidence in D'Alenquer must have been extremely high. Paulo da Gama captained the second ship, the *São Rafael.* Nicolau Coelho commanded the third and smallest ship, the *Berrio.*

Ship makers in Portugal developed the caravel in the fifteenth century. The caravel's smaller size allowed it to be sailed swiftly in the oceans.

Da Gama chose between 140 and 170 crewmen to work the ships. For the expedition, he selected only the most worthy seamen. He reviewed each man's land and sea conduct to make his decision. Whenever he could, he employed members of Diaz's crew, hoping to use their knowledge and experience. During the voyage, the ships would stop at ports where Portuguese was not spoken. Therefore, da Gama chose three interpreters for the mission. Martin Affonso was familiar with various African tribes and would help communicate with villagers along the African coast. Fernão Martins and João Nunes both spoke Arabic. They could

The Portuguese Caravel

In the late 1400s, Portuguese ship makers developed the caravel. This type of ship was used by Portugal and Spain for the next 300 years. The Portuguese created the vessel especially for exploring the African coast. Vasco da Gama and his men made their epic voyage in a caravel.

The caravel was about 65 feet long, which was smaller than previous ships. Because of its smaller size, the caravel could swiftly sail the ocean. Also, unlike earlier vessels, caravels could sail into the wind, or windward. This feature made the ship less dependent on wind currents to interpret the languages spoken by Muslims in India. Aside from navigators and sailors, da Gama commissioned soldiers, gunners, carpenters, and sail and rope makers. He also employed cooks, cabin boys, and even a surgeon.

On da Gama's request, the fleet also carried about 10 convicted prisoners. These men had committed serious crimes and were condemned to death. Da Gama wanted them for treacherous missions. At various stops in unknown territory,

carry it where it needed to go. The vessel was rigged with three or four masts. Only the foremast carried a square sail. All of the others had triangular, or lateen, sails.

Engineers designed the caravel with an improved sea structure. Wooden planks that made up the hull were thicker and stronger. Therefore, the hull was less likely to split and leak. The caravel had a broad bow and a high, narrow poop deck. This deck is the raised section at the rear of the ship. Caravels could carry up to 130 tons of cargo, which made them ideal trade ships.

he would send one of these men ashore to find food and water, locate villages, or gather other useful information. Da Gama even intended to leave a few men behind in these lands where they might be useful on his return. For those criminals who made it back, the king promised to grant full pardons for their faithful service.

The expedition to India might take as long as three years. Da Gama had to order food stores that would last the entire trip. Workers packed the ships with barrels of salt pork and beef, lentil beans, plums, onions, and honey. Sacks of salt, sugar, and flour lined the ships' shelves. The crew brought along gunpowder and crossbows, rope and extra sails.

At last all was ready. The vessels had been built, the crew was carefully selected, and food stores, fresh water, and equipment were loaded. Gazing at the handsome ships, the seamen itched with anticipation of their departure. All that was left was to wait for da Gama's formal sailing instructions from newly crowned King Manuel. The king called for a ceremony at a stoic, old castle in Montemó o Noro, a city 18 miles west of Lisbon. Government officers, nobles, and church leaders gathered for the grand occasion. King Manuel announced to the crowd, "I have chosen [Vasco da Gama] for this journey, as a loyal cavalier, worthy of such an honorable enterprise . . ."

Kneeling before the king, da Gama kissed his majesty's outstretched hand. "I, Vasco da Gama, who now have been commanded by you, most high and most powerful king," he said, "to set out to discover the seas and the lands of India . . . shall serve with all fidelity, loyalty, watchfulness, and diligence."[4] The ceremony concluded, and the great adventure waited for da Gama a few days later.

TO THE HORIZON

On Saturday, July 8, 1497, da Gama and his crews boarded the three vessels docked in Lisbon. The freshly painted ships looked bold and fearless standing in the sparkling water, bright flags snapping in the wind. Sailors stood tall in their tight cotton shirts, loose pants, and red caps. Crowds gathered along the shore to bid farewell to the brave men embarking on a dangerous journey. Handkerchiefs and scarves fluttered above the sea of townspeople. Women cried as they waved goodbye.

Da Gama peered out across the crowd with sober eyes. Some sailors thought they saw him shed a tear, which he quickly brushed away. Da Gama understood the importance of this mission. The da Gama reputation rode on his success or failure. In all his years at sea, da Gama had never lost a ship. This expedition would be no exception. With broad shoulders steady and a strong-set chin, he ordered the trumpets to sound. The blaring horns drowned out the sounds of weeping women. The anchor chains jangled as the weights lifted out of the water. Seamen hurried to raise the sails. As if by da Gama's order, a strong wind rose and bellied out the canvas sails. The fleet was on its way.

One week later, the fleet spotted the Canary Islands off the West African coast. There the crew dropped fishing nets into the water for some fresh food. That night, dense fog and strong winds rolled in, and the ships drifted apart. When the fog lifted the next morning, the *São Gabriel* had lost one of its mates—the *São Rafael.* Da Gama ordered the captain to continue to the coast in hopes of reconnecting with the lost ship. Although his face showed no worries, da Gama prayed for his brother's crew.

On July 22, a lookout spotted the *São Rafael.* Relieved, da Gama continued his journey down the African coast. The boats pushed past miles of low shores and sandy banks. The crew's next stop was at the Cape Verde Islands.

There, da Gama sent men ashore to search for fresh water, fruit, and vegetables. Men chopped firewood for the cooking stoves. The crewmen were surprised that da Gama ordered them to get so many barrels of water and extra stores of wood. They thought they would be making regular stops along the coastline.

Back on the ships, da Gama ordered the pilots to steer west, away from the coast. This decision seemed strange to Captain Álvares and many of the other seamen. As long as these sailors had known, boats always steered along the African coast as they headed south. On this route, the ships fought against the winds and currents. Da Gama believed that if the ships sailed out into the Atlantic and then eastward, the winds would carry them swiftly to the southern tip of Africa. D'Alenquer understood this route. It was similar to the navigation Diaz had taken nine years earlier. As it turned out, da Gama's

The town of Goree Island is on the Atlantic coast of Senegal. Da Gama's expedition followed the African coast for a while. Then it sailed west out into the Atlantic, hoping to catch winds that would take it around the southern tip of Africa.

decision was a good one. He had found the best and fastest route to the Cape of Good Hope.

The trip out to sea was tiresome for the crew. They battled fierce tempests and endless days with no land in sight. Finally, on November 1, the look-out yelled, "Land ho!" After more than three months in the mid-Atlantic, land was a fantastic sight. The ships drew closer together, and da Gama ordered the flags raised and salutes fired. That night, the crews celebrated their safe arrival at the African coast. They did not let their thoughts dwell on the greater troubles that awaited them.

Test Your Knowledge

1 How did a caravel differ from prior sailing vessels?

a. It was larger and heavier than other ships.

b. It was reinforced with iron plates and beams.

c. It was wider, with level decks and a flat bottom.

d. None of the above.

2 What languages did da Gama's interpreters speak?

a. German, French, and Arabic

b. Arabic and African dialects

c. Greek and Latin

d. None of the above

3 Why did da Gama include convicted prisoners in his crew?

a. He knew they would be hard workers.

b. He planned to send them on treacherous missions.

c. The king had ordered these men to be executed at sea.

d. None of the above.

4 What happened to the ship *São Rafael* in the Canary Islands?

a. It sank in a storm and was never found.

b. It was captured by pirates and burned.

c. It was lost in a storm but soon found.

d. None of the above.

5 Why did da Gama order his ships to sail away from the African coast?

a. He secretly wished to go to the Americas.

b. He was hoping to avoid pirates.

c. The winds along the coast were against him.

d. He knew the currents farther from the coast would prove quicker.

ANSWERS: 1. c; 2. b; 3. b; 4. c; 5. d

Along
Africa

After examining the ship readings, da Gama was a bit perplexed. In those days, sailors mapped their route by measuring the horizon and the position of the sun, moon, and stars. With the ship tossing and pitching on the waves, instrument readings were often unreliable. A ship could easily sail off course. While the crewmen made repairs and gathered wood and water, da Gama went on shore to make more accurate calculations.

Two sailors wandered farther into the island to explore. They spotted two African natives nearby. The natives were searching for honey, hunched over some bushes and holding smoking torches to drive the bees away. The crewmen ran back and told da Gama what they had seen. Da Gama ordered them to bring the natives to him. Maybe they could give him information about the unknown coast.

The sailors jumped out from behind some trees and grabbed the natives by surprise. One of them managed to escape. The captured native was terrified. He had never seen white men before. Their heavy clothes, long hair, and beards must have looked frightening to him. The native looked strange to da Gama's men, too. He was dressed only in an animal-skin loincloth.

An interpreter tried to talk to the native, but the two men didn't understand each other. The native was sobbing hysterically and could not even use signs to communicate. Da Gama called a cabin boy to take the native aboard the ship, and the cooks fed him a large meal. After a hearty feast, the man calmed down. Da Gama then used signs to talk to him. The man pointed to some mountains in the center of the island. His village was at the bottom of those mountains. Da Gama dressed the man in Portuguese clothes and sent him back to his village with gifts of bells and glass beads. Perhaps he would bring others to come and meet the sailors.

Da Gama guessed right. The next morning, the man reappeared with 15 more natives. They accepted more presents from the explorers and returned again to their village. Two days later, a group of about 50 natives gathered on shore. They brought shell earrings and foxtail fans to trade with the sailors.

One of da Gama's men, Fernand Veloso, wanted to go back to the natives' village to see how they lived. Da Gama thought Veloso was loud and obnoxious. He worried that such a visit would cause trouble for the explorers. But Veloso continued to plead with him until da Gama finally gave in. Da Gama watched the group of men walk away, laughing and chatting with each other.

Meanwhile, da Gama's brother Paulo decided to take some men offshore to hunt for whales. He had seen several young whales come near the shore for food. The men grabbed two harpoons, and Paulo foolishly tied the ends of the rope to the bow of their small boat, or shallop. As one of the whales swam by, a sailor speared it with his harpoon. The whale thrashed about wildly and swam out toward sea. The coiled line pulled tight, and the boat lunged forward, almost capsizing.

Paulo shouted for someone to give him a knife, so he could cut the rope. The men looked around at each other. No one had brought a knife. The boat continued to dip and rock, cutting into a trail of bloody, foaming water.

"We're doomed," a sailor cried. Just then, the whale turned around and headed back toward shore. It struck bottom and laid still. Paulo quickly untied the rope, and rowed the boat to safety.

Suddenly, Veloso came running down a hill toward the beach. He was calling out and making wild gestures with his arms. Vasco da Gama saw that something was wrong and yelled to the others to pick him up. As the shallop neared the shore, two natives ran down the hill after Veloso. Still others followed after them shooting at Veloso with bows and arrows. The two natives finally caught up to Veloso and tried to grab him. Luckily, he was good with his fists and fought them off. He quickly jumped into the shallop.

Da Gama, who was watching from on deck, set off in another boat. He speedily rowed to help his men. Arrows rained down on the sailors, and several were hit. Da Gama stood up in his boat and tried to make peace with the natives. Just then, an arrow pierced his leg. Since the sailors were unarmed, da Gama ordered his men to return to the main ships at once.

No one knows exactly what Veloso did to upset the native Africans. Regardless, the fight made it impossible for da Gama and his men to stay anchored in the bay. Fortunately, the crew had gathered plenty of fresh water, wood, and lobsters to set sail. Da Gama was still unsure where he was. He guessed he was near the Cape of Good Hope and set a course south-southwest. Two days later, the lookout shouted, "Land in sight on the port bow!"[5] There laid the welcome sight of the cape. At noon

The Cape of Good Hope is located at the southern tip of Africa. Almost five months after the expedition began, da Gama's fleet rounded the cape in November 1497.

on November 22, the ships rounded the point and sailed on their way along the coast. They had finally passed the landmark they had been striving to reach for almost five months. More important, da Gama's navigational skills won the respect and confidence of his crew—a feat that would come in very handy during the months ahead.

UP THE COAST

Da Gama and his crew sailed three more days along the coast. The three ships anchored in Mossel Bay. About 100 natives gathered on the shore to greet them. Da Gama and some of his men took a boat to shore, this time armed with guns in case of a surprise attack. As the boat neared shore, da Gama threw out small, tinkling bells to the natives. They danced with joy as they caught them. After picking a safe location, da Gama landed the boat. He traded red caps and more bells for ivory bracelets.

Two days later, almost 200 more Africans arrived. Again, da Gama and some of the crew took a boat to shore. This time, the natives were in a festive mood. They began playing wooden flutes. Soon, the Africans formed a dancing circle. Da Gama tapped his foot to the music. He waved a signal to the ship for the trumpets to play. After a while, da Gama and the sailors returned to the ship. The musicians onboard joined the trumpets in a light tune. All the crew jumped up and started dancing. Even da Gama began to celebrate. They had much to rejoice about—braving the wild Atlantic and rounding the Cape of Good Hope without much trouble.

Believing his stop to be a success, da Gama set up a stone pillar called a *padrão* on the shore. He also pounded wooden crosses into the ground. All Portuguese explorers placed padrãoes on land they had visited. It was their way of claiming the land for the Portuguese king. The monuments angered the natives. They understood them to be a symbol of ownership. From the ship deck, da Gama watched the Africans destroy the pillar and smash the crosses. Again, the explorers set sail under unfriendly terms.

Da Gama continued his voyage along the coast. Days of calm weather were followed by terrifying storms. The ships violently rocked while waves pounded against the hulls. On December 16, the fleet passed the last pillar set up by Diaz. They ventured into waters that no Portuguese sailor had ever seen. By Christmas, da Gama and his men had traveled more than 200 miles beyond the point where Diaz's men forced him to turn back. This area of the African coast is now called Natal—the Portuguese word for Christmas.

After being at sea for eight days straight, the crew's water supply was running low. Each man

By Christmas Day 1497, da Gama's expedition had traveled more than 200 miles farther than Bartholomew Diaz had sailed nine years before. Today, this area of the South African coast is called Natal, the Portuguese word for Christmas.

received less than a pint a day, and the cooks used seawater for all the cooking. Because the crew needed fresh water, da Gama told the pilot to find a spot to drop anchor. On January 11, 1498, the fleet anchored at the mouth of a small river.

Da Gama and some men rowed ashore. A large number of Africans again rushed to greet the Portuguese sailors. Unlike the other natives da Gama had met, these Africans had seen Europeans before. The interpreter Martin Affonso could understand the natives' language. When he found that the chief was friendly, da Gama offered gifts of a jacket, red trousers, a cap and a bracelet. The chief invited Affonso to his village. There, the sailor feasted on chicken and porridge made from a grain called millet. Affonso spent the night in the chief's hut.

The next morning, the chief gave Affonso some dead birds as a gift. Then, two Africans escorted the interpreter back to the shore. Apparently, news about the Portuguese explorers traveled to neighboring villages. Before long, about 200 natives crowded the beach. They brought casks of fresh water to the ship. Da Gama was pleased to find these natives so friendly. But a good sailing wind came up, and the sailors had to say goodbye to their new friends.

On January 25, the fleet anchored at the mouth of the Quelimane River, where the crew met more friendly natives. Two African chiefs paddled out to

Portuguese Maritime League

No, the Portuguese Maritime League (PML) was not a sponsor of boat races. It was a method to measure distance that was used by Portuguese sailors like Vasco da Gama. In the fifteenth century, sailors measured distance in leagues. Today, a league is considered equal to three miles. But in da Gama's day, there were many different measurements for a mile in Europe. The PML was equal to 3.2 nautical miles.

A nautical mile differs from a mile on land. One nautical mile equals about 1.15 land miles. A nautical mile is based on the circumference of the Earth. Imagine the Earth cut in half. In one half, the equator looks like a circle of 360 degrees. Each degree is divided into sixty minutes of arc. One minute of arc is equal to one nautical mile. At the equator the distance around the Earth is 21,600 nautical miles, or 24,857 land miles.

the main ship. Again, da Gama offered them gifts of clothing. His presents did not seem to impress the chiefs. Da Gama noticed one of the chiefs was wearing a valuable silk-trimmed hat. Through hand signs, the chiefs told him that they had seen large ships like the Portuguese ships before. Da Gama certainly thought he was close to India. Traders from the East had visited the natives.

The ships stayed anchored there for 32 days. Carpenters repaired a broken mast on the *São Rafael* and caulked the hulls. During the fierce ocean storms, the mast had snapped and the hulls had sprung leaks. While anchored, scurvy broke out among the men. Today, people understand that this disease is caused by a lack of vitamin C. Back in the 1400s, sailors were unsure what caused the deadly illness. The sailors' gums became swollen with foul, black blood. They could barely eat or drink. In time, their legs and arms also swelled and turned black and rotten, leaving them unable to move. If a sailor did not get fresh fruit or vegetables in time, he would surely die. Luckily, some of the sailors bartered with the natives for fresh food, and the scurvy disappeared.

Finally, on February 24, the fleet again set sail. Da Gama was so focused on his royal mission that he had no idea what he was leaving behind. The land of southern Africa was rich in agriculture, minerals and diamonds. One day, this land would become a center of European colonization. But for now, da Gama cared only about getting to India. He and his ships sailed northeast for 300 miles between Africa and Madagascar, until they spotted the island of Moçambique.

Test Your Knowledge

1 What did da Gama use to determine his expedition's position at sea?

a. A compass

b. The sun, moon, and stars

c. Wind speed

d. None of the above

2 What did Fernand Veloso do to offend the African villagers?

a. He refused their gifts of food and spices.

b. He insulted their leader.

c. He tried to take a villager as a slave.

d. We don't know.

3 What is a *padrão*?

a. A weapon da Gama used to defend himself against the African villagers

b. A small sailing vessel, like a launch

c. A stone pillar erected to claim a territory

d. None of the above

4 How did da Gama know that the Africans at the Quelimane River had seen Indian traders?

    a. They used weapons the traders had given them.

    b. One of the chiefs was wearing a silk-trimmed hat.

    c. One of the chiefs offered da Gama Indian spices and herbs.

    d. None of the above.

5 What is scurvy and how is it caused?

    a. It is a disease caused by a lack of vitamin C.

    b. It is a blood disease spread by animal bites.

    c. It is a virus spread by mosquitoes.

    d. None of the above.

ANSWERS: 1. b; 2. d; 3. c; 4. b; 5. a

Trouble in Mozambique

On the morning of March 2, Vasco da Gama's fleet neared the city of Moçambique in Mozambique. This flourishing commerce center was the first of several Arab settlements along the East Coast of Africa. Many foreign ships filled the port. Traders were busy loading and unloading crates of exotic spices, like cloves, ginger, or pepper. Some ships transported gold, silver, pearls, and other precious stones. Wealthy merchants carried cargo between India, Persia, Malaya, the East Indies, China, Arabia, and Africa. Moçambique was the busiest city of Arab-controlled trade. The ships pulling in and out of the bustling port were masters of the Indian Ocean.

To da Gama, the scattered Arab towns represented a religion that had rivaled Christianity for hundreds of years—Islam. The Muslims had been hostile to the Christians. If da Gama told the inhabitants who he was, he risked being attacked. Luckily, the townspeople believed da Gama and his men were Muslims. And for protection, da Gama did not correct them.

Da Gama now faced a more difficult challenge— dealing with the people of the Eastern African waters. He began to show a quick and violent temper. He used poor judgment and sometimes, cruelty. His actions would affect the future of his country in relations with Africa and Asia. Da Gama placed mistrust and fear into the hearts of many Arab traders, a move that would curse his fellow explorers and traders for centuries.

The local ruler, or sheik, approached the vessels, riding in two covered canoes that had been tied together. The sheik, Sultan Khwaza, was wearing a pleated velvet jacket, wrapped in a blue cloak that hung to his knees. He wore loose, white, ankle-length pants. A silk sash was tied around his waist. A silver dagger and a shiny sword hung from his belt. On top of his velvet cap, he wore a colorful silk turban decorated with gold braids. Nicolau Coelho, the captain of the *Berrio*, invited the sheik onto his ship.

To this extravagantly dressed man, Coelho offered a plain red hood. Despite the insulting gift, the sheik invited some of the Portuguese sailors—who he believed were Muslims—back to his home. He served them food and drinks. The sheik visited da Gama's vessel several times, bringing gifts of dates and expensive spices. Da Gama made the same mistake as Coelho and gave the sheik trashy gifts of hats, garments, and strings of coral. Perhaps da Gama did not have any gifts appropriate for such a royal guest. But the cheap presents made da Gama look ungrateful and made a bad impression on the ruler.

While they were anchored, the Portuguese met two Christian captives. They were taken aboard the *São Gabriel.* As soon as the captives saw the painted figurehead of the angel Gabriel, they fell to their knees in worship. The Muslims noticed that da Gama and the other crew members were happy to talk with these despised Christians. They wondered if the Portuguese were really Christians themselves. They dragged the captives back to shore, and da Gama never saw them again. The Muslims told the sheik about their suspicions.

Meanwhile, da Gama continued to prepare for the voyage across the Indian Ocean. He again invited the Moçambique ruler onboard for a meal. Da Gama had no idea the sheik knew the crewmen were Christians. And the sheik did not let on. During dinner, da Gama asked if he could hire two pilots to help him navigate across the unknown Indian Ocean. The ruler agreed to help him find navigators, as long as the pilots accepted da Gama's terms. Da Gama offered the pilots 30 gold matikals (about $90) and two marlotes (short silk cloaks worn in India). He paid them right away so the men could leave support for their families. But da Gama

This manuscript shows da Gama's three ships. While sailing along the African coast, da Gama wanted to find locals to help him navigate across the Indian Ocean, which was unknown to him.

did not trust the men. He told them that if one of them wanted to go ashore, the other had to remain on the ship.

Over the next few days, the locals learned that da Gama's men were Christians. Frequent clashes arose between the townspeople and the sailors landing for food, wood, and water. Da Gama decided it would be better if the fleet retreated out of the bay. On March 10, da Gama ordered the crew to draw off to São Jorge Island, a few miles out of the port. At some point, one pilot had sneaked ashore and not returned. With two boats of men and the other pilot, da Gama set out to find him. As the boats rowed toward town, five Arab dugout vessels headed out from shore. Each dugout was filled with armed men holding bows, long arrows, and shields.

Da Gama immediately grabbed the other pilot, so he would not try to escape. He ordered the men to fire bombards, or cannons, at the approaching Arabs. When Paulo—who was on the *Berrio*—heard the firing, he set sail toward the enemy dugouts. But the Arabs fled in confusion and beached their boats before Paulo came within firing range.

Frustrated, da Gama returned to the main ship. The whole fleet took up the coast. Fortunately, they had plenty of wood, vegetables, birds, and goats, and a limited supply of water. Da Gama breathed a sigh of relief in escaping a dangerous situation. But he was congratulating himself too soon.

By March 13, the fleet had sailed only 20 leagues up the coast. The wind dropped, forcing the crew to stop, and it remained calm for two days. Anxious to keep moving, da Gama commanded the pilots to pull farther off shore in hopes of catching a good wind. Instead, they got caught in a backward current. By morning, the current had carried them a distance below Moçambique.

Again, da Gama waited for favorable winds to pick up. The ships remained anchored for eight days. The crew's water supply began running low, and it was necessary to land once more near Moçambique. The Arab pilot still on board promised to show the Portuguese where to find water without danger. That night, under the cover of darkness, da Gama and Coelho led the ships' shallops to shore. The pilot— perhaps hoping to escape—led the men aimlessly through the dark. The group never came to any water. In the morning, da Gama and his men returned to the ships with empty casks.

The following night, another group went out with the pilot. Finally, they found a watering spot. Suddenly, an army of the sheik's men ran onto the beach and ordered the men off. Da Gama knew how important it was to get water. He ordered his men to fire bombards at the natives, forcing them to retreat into the woods. Da Gama landed his crew, and they filled their water casks.

In the early morning of March 24, a boat of natives rowed out to da Gama's ship. They yelled at him to stop trying to land for any more water.

Da Gama's temper flared. He would not let the Arabs threaten him. He could do whatever he pleased. He shouted for all men to be on deck. He ordered his men to arm the boats with bombards and lower them at once.

Meanwhile, an army of natives gathered on the beach, carrying swords, bows, and slingshots. As da Gama's men neared the shore, they attacked the boats with a shower of stones from their slings.

Da Gama commanded his men to fire the bombards. Shots boomed from the cannons. The

Arabs quickly retreated into a wooden fort. The fort was little protection from the stone cannonballs. During three hours of fighting, two natives were killed—one on the beach and the other inside the fort. Da Gama's men tired of the battle, and returned to the ship for lunch.

On March 27, the fleet set sail again for São Jorge. Before raising anchor, da Gama ordered a few more bombards fired at the town, just for good measure. At São Jorge, the crew again waited for a favorable wind. The wind picked up on March 28. But after sailing just three days and 20 leagues up coast, the winds dropped.

The Arab pilot caused much trouble for da Gama. When he misidentified a group of islands, da Gama lost his temper. He had the man tied up and brutally flogged, or whipped. He thought the pilot was trying to get his ships lost. Perhaps he would have to find someone else to give them directions.

As they sailed up the coast, da Gama captured a small sailing vessel carrying an old Arab man and two Africans. At once, da Gama began torturing the old man for information about coastal towns. Da Gama was determined to get what he wanted. His cruelty showed no bounds in achieving his goals.

AMBUSHED AT MOMBASA

On April 7, the ships neared Mombasa, Kenya, the finest harbor on the East African coast. The rocky peninsula rose out of the sea, just like the Portuguese homeland. Some weary sailors mistook it for home. One sailor described it: "Its whitewashed stone houses had windows and terraces like those of Portugal and Spain. And it was so beautiful that some of our men felt as though they were entering some part of Portugal."[6]

The ruler at Mombasa had no doubt heard about the mischief da Gama had visited on Moçambique. As soon as the Portuguese ships came into sight, he sent a boat out to meet them. The messengers demanded that da Gama tell them who he was, where he came from, and where he was going. Da Gama—through his interpreter Fernão Martins—asked them for provisions. The natives promised friendship and guaranteed plenty of supplies. But da Gama suspected trouble.

All night, guards on each vessel stood watch. Sure enough, at midnight some natives started to climb up the side of the *São Gabriel.* Da Gama stopped them before they could make it on board. It was obvious to da Gama that the natives wanted to know if the Portuguese were ready for an attack.

The local sheik continued to lure da Gama. He offered sheep, oranges, lemons, and sugar cane. If da Gama came into port, the sheik vowed he would give da Gama everything he needed for his voyage. The next morning, da Gama's ships sailed into the harbor. Two of the ships accidentally collided, causing a moment of confusion. During the chaos, two Arab prisoners jumped overboard and swam to a nearby boat.

Da Gama flew into a terrible rage. He captured a native vessel and had the passengers dragged before him. He demanded to know what their ruler planned to do. The poor natives said they knew nothing. Da Gama tightened his lips and narrowed his eyes. He asked if an attack was planned, but the natives insisted they knew nothing.

Da Gama ordered his crew to bring him a basin of boiling water. For a moment, his crew stood in frozen silence. He screamed at them to bring it at once.

The men brought a fire with a bowl of boiling water over it. They stripped the two prisoners and

Crossing the Sandy Sea

Between the 600s and the 1000s, Arab armies began raiding North Africa. The Arab conquest helped create tremendous trade routes across the Sahara Desert. Trade also brought the Islamic faith and Arabic language, which still prevail in North Africa today.

The sands of the Sahara Desert could have been a major obstacle to trade among Africa, Europe, and Eastern countries like India and China. Instead, the desert was a sandy sea, with trade ports on either side. In the south, key "ports" were Timbuktu and Gao. An important northern city was Ghadames, in present-day Libya. From these places, goods traveled to Europe, Arabia, India, and China.

Muslim traders of North Africa sent goods across the Sahara Desert in large camel caravans. The caravans averaged about 1,000 camels. But some caravans were as large as 12,000 camels. Muslims mainly brought luxury items, like tied their hands behind their backs. Da Gama ordered one of his men to scoop a ladle of water out of the basin. Da Gama again asked about their ruler's plans. Once again, they denied all knowledge.

silks, textiles, beads, ceramics, and decorated weapons and utensils. They traded these goods for gold, ivory, cotton, copper, dates, olives, rich woods like ebony, and caffeine-containing kola nuts, which the Arabs used to perk up. Wanderers, or nomads, of the Sahara Desert traded salt and meat to passing caravans. They also sold their knowledge of the desert and served as guides to travelers. Another huge trade enterprise was slavery. Arab and Berber princes wanted slaves to use as servants, soldiers, and field workers.

Trade across the "sandy sea" connected West African culture to the Mediterranean world and eventually to Western Europe. Rumors of the wonderful treasure in West Africa reached Portugal. Portuguese explorers heard about fabulous Guinea where gold abounded. The tales sparked the interest of explorers, like Vasco da Gama, who set out to discover these glittering foreign lands.

Da Gama nodded at the crewman. He slowly poured the scalding water over the prisoners' skin. The natives twisted and shrieked in pain. Their skin immediately blistered and tore. All the while, da Gama fixed a cold stare on the prisoners.

Finally, the natives talked. The sheik planned to coax the vessels into the harbor. The attack, in revenge for the people of Moçambique, would come when da Gama was not on his guard, one prisoner gasped. Even after receiving the information, da Gama ordered yet another ladle of water poured over the men. One native wiggled free and threw himself over the ship railing into the harbor. The other prisoner also escaped into the water. A passing boat picked up both men.

Night fell, and da Gama alerted his ships to the treacherous plot. About midnight, natives sneaked up on the fleet. They stopped their boats a safe distance away and swam up to the *São Rafael* and the *Berrio*. The ship guards heard splashing in the water below. At first, they thought it was simply fish jumping out of the sea. But suddenly, the natives began slashing the anchor cables of the *Berrio*. Others scaled the side of the ship and swung at the masts with axes. "Attack!" the Portuguese sailors warned the other ships.

When the Mombasans realized that they were discovered, they slipped back into the water and swam to their boats. Once again, da Gama was forced to pull up anchor and draw back farther off shore.

FINALLY, AN ALLY

On April 14, da Gama's crew dropped anchor off Malindi, Kenya—about 30 leagues north of Mombasa. Here, da Gama at last found an ally. News of da Gama's attack had reached the sheik here, too. But the ruler of Malindi was an enemy of Mombasa. He believed the Portuguese were powerful and would make a strong ally. He promised to find good pilots for da Gama.

The next day, da Gama sent a prisoner to shore as a go-between for the sheik and himself. That evening, the man returned with a gift of three sheep and a message of friendship from the ruler. Da Gama sent him a cloak, two strings of coral, three wash basins, a hat, little bells, and two pieces of striped trade cloth. It was not much of a gift for the ruler of a rich, independent city, but it was a better present than da Gama had given the other rulers.

The sheik responded with more generous gifts. Da Gama watched the loaded dugout boats near the ship. Messengers brought six sheep, cloves, cumin, ginger, nutmeg, and pepper. Also, the ruler of Malindi offered to meet with da Gama on his ship. In this way, da Gama could feel protected. After dinner, Vasco waited on deck for the sheik. Finally, the sheik and his son arrived. The ruler wore a rich, damask robe lined with green satin and an elaborate headpiece. He sat on a cushioned chair made of bronze. Musicians accompanied the sheik on his boat. They played beautifully carved trumpets of ivory and wood.

The meeting was a remarkable success. The sheik agreed to replenish da Gama's supplies and recruit a knowledgeable navigator. A week of festivities and friendly visits followed. After a week, da Gama became impatient. Too much time was being wasted on frivolous celebration. When the sheik's servant rowed out to the *São Gabriel*, da Gama held him hostage. He sent a message to the sheik, demanding his pilot at once. Worried about losing his new allies,

Da Gama erected this stone cross at Malindi, Kenya. Here, da Gama had found an ally—the ruler of Malindi was an enemy of Mombasa.

the sheik immediately sent da Gama a pilot. In turn, da Gama released the servant.

As it turned out, the pilot was a master navigator. Pilot Ahmad ibn Majid could easily guide the fleet over the unknown Indian Ocean. With water casks filled, provisions stocked, and plenty of wood, da Gama gave the order to raise anchor on April 24. The broad white sails with great red crosses bellied out in the wind. And the fleet of Vasco da Gama embarked on its last stage of the voyage to India.

Test Your Knowledge

1 Why did da Gama allow the inhabitants of Moçambique to believe that he and his crew were Muslims?

a. He hoped to get a better price on spices.

b. He was concerned that he and his crew might be attacked.

c. He planned to convert to the Islamic faith.

d. None of the above.

2 How did da Gama manage to insult Sultan Khwaza?

a. He presented the sultan with cheap and meager gifts.

b. He told the sultan that the Portuguese were a Christian people.

c. He challenged the sultan to a display of swordsmanship.

d. None of the above.

3 How did da Gama show his cruelty when his crew ran short of fresh water?

a. He attacked the Arabs near Moçambique.

b. He had his Arab pilot flogged for giving incorrect directions.

c. He tortured an old man for information about coastal towns.

d. All of the above.

4 How did da Gama discover the plot to ambush him at Mombasa?

   a. He bribed local traders for information.

   b. He consulted a local fortune teller.

   c. He saw the coming ambush in a dream.

   d. He had two natives tortured with boiling water.

5 Why did the sheik of Malindi agree to help da Gama?

   a. He was an enemy of Mombasa and saw da Gama as a trading partner.

   b. He was hoping to trick da Gama and murder him.

   c. He was hoping to cheat da Gama out of his gold.

   d. None of the above.

ANSWERS: 1. b; 2. a; 3. d 4. d; 5. a

India!

The voyage across the Indian Ocean was uneventful. On May 20, 1498, the lookout spotted high land. After nearly 11 months, the long journey to India was over. The city of Calicut was the most important and richest commercial center on the Malabar Coast, the very southwest coast of India. The sole ruler of Calicut

71

was the samorin—from a Malayalam word meaning "lord of the sea." His prestige and wealth made him the most powerful ruler in all of Malabar. The samorin was a Hindu leader while many of the merchants in Calicut were Muslim. The samorin was soon to meet his match, a Portuguese explorer whose fame was only being discovered. His ships had just dropped anchor that evening of May 20.

IN CALICUT

The anchors had barely hit the water when four small boats approached the fleet. The men on board asked da Gama his nationality. He answered their questions, and the boats rowed back to shore. Fishing boats surrounded the fleet. The crew was extremely anxious to set foot on shore. The long 26-day trip from Malindi had made them restless. In celebration of their arrival, the men sang and danced into the early hours of the morning.

Sunrise was just breaking when the same boats from the day before appeared at the ladder of da Gama's ship. Da Gama wasted no time in completing his plans. He sent one of his men who spoke Arabic and Hebrew back to shore with the boats.

"Pay close attention," da Gama told him. "I want to know all you see and hear."

The natives took the sailor to the house of two Arabs who spoke his language. The greeting by the Arabs was rude. "The devil take you!" they shouted. "What brought you here?"[7]

"We come in search of Christians and spices," the sailor answered. Seeing the sailor did not want to fight, the Arabs calmed down. They served him wheat bread and honey to eat. Then, the sailor returned to the ship with one of his hosts.

Apparently, the Arab host was more concerned with making a profit than with politics. "A lucky venture, a lucky venture!" he exclaimed to the commander. "Plenty of rubies, plenty of emeralds! You owe great thanks to God for having brought you to a country possessing such riches!"[8] The host then told da Gama that the samorin was away in Panane—a coastal town 28 miles south of Calicut. When the commander heard this news, he sent Fernão Martins and another Portuguese interpreter to Panane with a message for His Majesty. Two ambassadors of the king of Portugal had come to Calicut. The samorin sent a message to da Gama in which he announced his return to the city. He also sent da Gama a present of fine cloth.

No doubt the samorin was sincere in his welcome and friendship to da Gama. The prosperity of his realm depended on commerce. It was to his advantage to open up many channels of trade between

Life in Calicut

At the time da Gama arrived, Calicut was a bustling city. Houses crowded down to the water's edge. Little red crabs scurried along the muddy banks, and crocodiles hid in the shallow waters. Merchants flooded the narrow, winding streets, while monkeys swung from tall coconut trees overhead. Yellow parakeets dotted the rooftops like pieces of sun dropped from the sultry sky. It was a bizarre and beautiful sight to da Gama's crew.

Just after their arrival, while anchored in the bay, da Gama's sailors leaned on their ships' bulwarks and watched a strange new way of fishing. The fishermen held torches and lanterns over the water. Fish—attracted by the light—leaped right into the low-sided boats. The Portuguese sailors marveled at this effortless method.

India and Europe. However, the Muslim merchants worried that the Europeans would steal their profits. They made a secret plot to turn the samorin against the Portuguese.

Da Gama helped the Muslims along. He told the natives that not only was he an ambassador of King

Inside the city, confusion bubbled from each corner. Rows of every kind of shop lined the streets. There were fruit stands with lemons, oranges, mangoes, and bunches of bananas. Sea merchants watched over stalls of fresh-caught fish. The aromas of wild spices, perfumes, and roasted nuts hung in the thick air. Dealers of precious stones sat beside scales on their mats, surrounded by tiny packets of diamonds, sapphires, rubies, emeralds, garnets, turquoise, and the coveted cat's-eye. The shops were visited by many buyers from distant lands—Hindus, Arabs, Persians, Syrians, Turks, Chinese, and tall dark-skinned Somalis. Different languages were heard on every side. Yet the marketplace was always peaceful and controlled.

Manuel, but that he was part of a much larger fleet. He claimed he had separated from the other ships during a voyage that lasted two years. Although he did not yet realize it, da Gama had made a foolish blunder. News of his clashes on the East African coast had already begun to trickle into Calicut. His false claims branded him a liar right from the start. Da Gama's continued arrogance laid a foundation of hard feelings that would last for many years.

On the morning of May 28, da Gama assembled an envoy of 13 men to go ashore and visit the king. The officers and crew dressed in their finest clothes. Other crew members prepared the boat, decorating it with flags and loading it with bombards–in case of a conflict. Vasco left Paulo in command of the ships during his absence. Before climbing down the ladder into the boat, Vasco turned to the crew. He spoke in calm, even tones, saying that if something unfortunate happened and he did not return, the crew should set sail at once for Portugal, and give an account of the voyage to the king. Then, he climbed down the ladder. As the men stepped into the boats, the fleet's guns fired a salute and the crewmen raised flags and banners on the mast.

Vasco da Gama presents a letter from the king of Portugal to the samorin of Calicut.

On the shore, the king had ordered a huge welcoming reception for the Portuguese. Da Gama noticed that most of the men were armed. The natives took da Gama and his men to Capua, a town about seven miles from Calicut. There, they were served a meal of fish and buttered rice. After eating, the men took boats down the Elatur River to Calicut.

In the city, the first place da Gama's men visited was a temple. The Portuguese knew very little about the Hindu religion. In the temple, they mistook a statue for the Virgin Mary. For their entire stay, the men thought the people were Christians, like them, and the temples were churches. The procession left the temple, followed by an escort of the king's servants and musicians. The musicians walked alongside the newcomers, beating drums and blowing bagpipes. One of da Gama's men wrote, "They showed us much respect, more than is shown in Spain to a king."[9] Crowds gathered in the streets. People leaned out their windows and climbed onto the roofs to watch the colorful king's procession. At the palace gate, the escort had to force its way through the tightly packed crowd of people in order to make a path.

The entire day was spent on the journey from the ships to the palace. The samorin met da Gama and his men in a small palace courtroom. He sat on a couch covered in green velvet. Da Gama entered the court and saluted the exalted king. He clasped his hands together and raised them up, in the same way he had seen the Indian people greet each other. The samorin invited the men to sit down. Servants washed their hands and presented them with a platter of sliced (jack) fruit and bananas— fruits they had never tasted before.

Through an interpreter, the samorin asked da Gama the purpose of his voyage. Da Gama told the ruler that King Manuel of Portugal had heard great things about India, especially of Calicut. King Manuel admires the ingenuity of the people of Calicut, da Gama praised. He said he had been sent to make an alliance that would benefit both lands. The samorin was gracious in his reply. He welcomed da Gama and his men into the city and extended his hand in friendship.

Da Gama and his men spent the night in the city in one of the king's houses. When da Gama arrived at the house, he found his own bed had been carried off the ship and set up in his room. Also there were the gifts that da Gama planned to give the samorin.

The next morning, da Gama asked the samorin's officers to come to his room and inspect the gifts he had brought for the king. They stared in astonishment at the miserable things set out. The goods were fit for a petty chief, but would be an insult to the wealthy lord of Calicut. Da Gama had laid out twelve pieces of striped cloth, four scarlet hoods, six hats, four strings of coral, six wash basins, a case of sugar, two casks of oil, and two casks of honey. One of the Arab officers laughed at the proposed gifts and refused to take them to the samorin. "The poorest merchant from Mecca or any part of India gave more," he said. "If you want to make a present it should be in gold. The king will not accept such meager things." [10]

Embarrassed, da Gama lied again. He told the officers that the gifts were his own personal possessions. If the king of Portugal let him return, he would send far richer presents. But still the officers refused to take the presents to the samorin. At this response, da Gama demanded to speak with the king. The officers promised to return shortly and take him to the palace. Da Gama waited all day, his impatience turning to burning anger. He considered storming into the palace alone, but finally decided against it. Da Gama's men were not much help in the matter. They wandered here and there throughout the city, acting more like tourists than explorers on a mission.

The next day, May 30, the officers at last returned. They brought the commander and his men to the palace. Again, da Gama was kept waiting, "fuming and fretting," outside a door. Finally, he and two of his men were allowed inside. Da Gama chose his interpreter Fernão Martins and his secretary. This time, the samorin was short in his conversation and less friendly to the Portuguese. The exchange of gifts on such an occasion was so common that da Gama's failure to bring suitable gifts angered the king. Also, the intelligent Muslims of Calicut already sensed the threat of European traders. They started rumors about da Gama, calling him a bloody-minded pirate.

Of course, the samorin knew nothing about the Portuguese. All he had heard were the stories of violence that came before them. He valued the Muslim people. After all, it was the Arabs who had built up his city. Naturally, he chose to believe them. Unfortunately, he should have trusted the Europeans. From that time forward, Calicut declined in wealth and importance.

The samorin bluntly stated that the lack of presents was very displeasing. He then suggested that da Gama give him the golden image of Santa Maria from his ship. Da Gama replied that the figure was

Vasco da Gama meets with the samorin of Calicut, India, in his palace.

not made of gold, only painted wood. Da Gama then described the products of Portugal—gold, silver, coral beads, and scarlet cloth, of which he had samples. He asked to return to the ships for them, while several of his men stayed behind with the king. The samorin flatly refused. He instructed him to take all of his men back, land his merchandise, and sell it if he was able. Because it was late at night, the Portuguese spent another night in their quarters.

The following morning, da Gama and his crew set out for their boats. On the way to the anchorage, the men became separated. By the time they reunited, darkness had fallen and a gusty wind blew. Da Gama requested a boat to take him to the ships, but the wali, or samorin's officer, refused to give him one. Da Gama immediately suspected that the samorin was trying to capture and destroy the fleet. He sent messengers out in different directions to warn Coelho and Paulo. The commander and the rest of the men found lodging at the house of a Muslim trader.

The next day, da Gama again asked for a boat. The wali told him he could have a boat if he agreed to anchor the fleet closer to shore. Da Gama vehemently refused and demanded to speak to the samorin personally. At this request, the officers locked da Gama and his men in the house and kept them under close guard.

Later, the guards made da Gama an offer. If he surrendered his sails and rudders, he could return to his ships. Without this equipment, the ships would be useless. Of course, da Gama did not agree to the deal.

Da Gama then tried to bargain with the officers. He agreed to stay a prisoner if his men could go free.

"They will stay right where they are," the guards replied.

"They will die of hunger," da Gama pleaded.

"If they die of hunger, they must bear it," the Arabs coldly announced. "It makes no difference to us."[11]

Meanwhile, the messenger whom da Gama had sent out found Captain Coelho and gave him the news. Coelho returned to the ships and kept them well-guarded.

Another day passed. Da Gama and his men were more closely guarded than ever. Over 100 men armed with swords, two-edged battle-axes, bows, arrows, and shields surrounded the house. On June 2, the wali ordered da Gama to have the Portuguese merchandise on his ship and the crews brought to land. The crews would not be returned to the vessels until all the items had been sold. The wali claimed that this action was the local custom.

Da Gama knew it would be foolish to surrender his crew. Instead, he sent a letter to Paulo. He instructed his brother to land certain items, but not all of the merchandise. As soon as Paulo landed, da Gama and his men were released. He left Diogo Dias and an assistant in charge of the landed goods. Back on board his ship, da Gama barked that no more merchandise would leave the ships.

After two months, da Gama had no success in selling his goods to the Muslims or the Hindus. He decided it was useless to remain on the coast. On August 9, he sent Dias to the samorin with gifts of amber, coral, and other items. Dias told the king that the Portuguese wished to sail for home. He asked if a representative of Calicut would accompany them back to Portugal. Da Gama also requested a gift of a bahar (204 kilograms) each of cinnamon and cloves, and samples of other spices for the king of Portugal. The samorin had no interest in the measly gifts. If da Gama wanted to leave, he would have to pay 600 xerafins (about $900) to leave his merchandise behind in the warehouse.

Da Gama was frustrated. Some of his men were now prisoners of the samorin. The fleet's departure seemed indefinitely delayed. Then, to make matters worse, da Gama heard rumors that the samorin had received large bribes to destroy the fleet and kill the Portuguese sailors.

On August 19, 25 Arabs rowed out to da Gama's ship. Da Gama gladly welcomed the visitors aboard. Suddenly, the commander ordered his men to seize some of them. He sent the other Arabs back to shore with a message for the samorin. The hostages would be released when the king returned his men and the merchandise.

After four days passed without any word, da Gama was ready to give up. He ordered the ships to set sail. He sent word to the king that he would return to Calicut and teach the people a lesson. The fleet had only sailed about 15 miles when it faced a strong headwind and had to drop anchor.

On August 26, a native boat approached the fleet. The man on board said Diogo Dias was at the samorin's palace. As soon as da Gama released the hostages, Dias would be returned to the boat. Vasco assumed Dias was already dead. He was too smart to fall for a trick. He believed the samorin wanted to keep the ships nearby until the Muslims could attack.

Da Gama ordered the native boat to go and to not return without Dias or a letter written in his handwriting. Again, he ordered the anchors weighed, or raised, and sailed a short distance down the coast.

When the samorin got news of da Gama's departure and threats, he was alarmed. He immediately sent for Dias. He assured Dias that it was his official who had demanded the 600 xerafins as custom duties, not him. Then, he kindly asked Dias to write a letter to the king of Portugal on a palm leaf—a sign of peace. The letter read: "Vasco da Gama, a gentleman of your household, came to my country, whereat I was pleased. My country is rich in cinnamon, cloves, ginger, pepper, and precious stones. That which I ask of you in exchange is gold, silver, corals, and scarlet cloth." [12]

He sent Dias and the other Portuguese men back to their ships. In turn, da Gama released six hostages and promised to surrender the others as soon as his merchandise was delivered. The next day, more boats appeared at da Gama's vessel. The Arabs promised to return the merchandise as soon as the remaining hostages were set free. Da Gama's temper had been tested to the limit.

He shouted at them to go away and said he would take the hostages to Portugal. He vowed to return and prove to the samorin that the Portuguese were not thieves as the Muslims had said.

On August 29, 1498, with samples of spices and precious stones, da Gama ordered the sails set and anchors weighed. As the fleet moved out, the Portuguese flag rose up the mast to the blast of trumpets and the roll of drums. The three ships that had made a historical voyage now turned their prows back toward Africa.

Test Your Knowledge

1 Who was the "samorin"?

a. An Arab spy placed aboard
da Gama's ship

b. An African tribal leader

c. The Hindu ruler of the city
of Calicut

d. A Muslim cleric

2 What was the first lie da Gama told
in Calicut?

a. That he had come seeking spices

b. That his ships were part of a
larger fleet

c. That he was not a Christian

d. None of the above

3 What gifts did da Gama attempt to present
to the samorin?

a. Scarlet hoods, hats, strings of coral,
wash basins, honey

b. Gold and silver trinkets he had stolen
from East Africa

c. Gold and silver he had brought from
King Manuel of Portugal

d. None of the above

4 How much Portuguese merchandise was da Gama able to sell in India?

a. All he had brought

b. About half of his supply

c. Almost none

d. Da Gama's merchandise never made it to shore

5 What ransom did the samorin demand, if da Gama was to leave his merchandise in the warehouse?

a. Ten gold bars and twenty silver bars

b. All the scarlet cloth aboard da Gama's ship

c. Da Gama's sails and rudder

d. Money equal to about $900 today

ANSWERS: 1. c; 2. b; 3. a; 4. c; 5. d

The Voyage Home

The voyage back to the African coast started with an event that could have met with a terrible end. At noon the day after setting sail, the wind suddenly calmed. The fleet was still very close to Calicut. About 70 boats quickly surrounded the ships. Vasco da Gama took action. He cleared the decks for battle, and when the boats came within range, he ordered his men to fire the bombards. Even with the cannon volleys, the boats continued to close in with incredible speed. Luckily, a thunderstorm rose in the clouds. The winds filled the sails and carried da Gama's fleet out to sea. Eventually, the boats turned back to Calicut. And da Gama escaped another dangerous conflict.

On September 10, da Gama released a hostage with a letter of peace to the samorin. He explained that he had carried the hostages so he could prove his discoveries to the king. The only reason he did not leave a representative in Calicut was that he worried the Muslims might kill him.

Near the end of September, the ships arrived at the Angediva Islands. The fleet anchored to gather wood, fresh water, and vegetables for the journey across the Indian Ocean. While the crews were at work, two large vessels neared the anchorage. The lookout called down from the masthead that he saw another six ships farther out at sea.

Da Gama feared his enemy was pursuing him. He ordered both vessels to be sunk. One ship escaped, and the other suffered a broken rudder. As the Portuguese came upon the damaged ship, its crew fled in the ship's boat. Da Gama's men climbed aboard but found only food, coconuts, palm sugar, and some weapons. Da Gama never learned exactly what the ships wanted, but he was sure they were sent to destroy the Portuguese.

The fleet remained in the Angediva Islands for 12 days. Before setting sail, the crew burned the captured vessel—even though its captain offered a good sum for its safe return. From October 2 to January 2, 1499, the ships crossed the Arabian Sea. The weather alternated between dead calm and backward winds. The trip took much longer than planned. All the vegetables were eaten up, the water became foul, other food ran low, and scurvy again attacked the crew. Thirty more men died of the disease. Even the iron-willed da Gama had to force himself to drive the others. He finally decided that if a favorable wind would carry them back to India, they would sail back to replenish their stores.

Fortunately, the sailor had a stroke of good luck. A favorable wind rose up and pushed them on their way. Six days later, the crew spotted land. Every man on board let out a cheer of relief.

On January 7, Malindi was sighted, and the weary sailors dropped anchor in a familiar spot. The townspeople welcomed them with sheep, oranges, eggs, and many other foods. Sadly, the food did not help the sick. The hot, humid weather at Malindi

The Chinese Junk

The Portuguese were not the only experienced sailors on the high seas. The Chinese developed one of the strongest and most seaworthy vessels ever built—the junk. This ship was like a large, lightweight, flat-bottomed box. The body of the ship, or the hull, was made up of watertight, fireproof compartments. These bulkheads made the junk structurally durable and protected it from sinking.

Because junks had flat bottoms, they did not have a keel. This wooden beam runs along the full length of the bottom of a ship. Most European ships had keels. If a ship capsized, it was said to have "keeled over." The keel cut through the water and helped steer the ship. Instead of a keel, junks had a heavy steering oar, or rudder, mounted in the bottom part of the ship. The rudder could be only made their illnesses worsen. More mariners died while anchored here. When da Gama realized how generous the sheik of Malindi was, he asked for more favors. He begged for a tusk of ivory to take back to the Portuguese king. He also asked if he

raised or lowered to steer the vessel. Junk sails were narrow, horizontal linen panels. Each thin sail was on its own retracting line so that it could be quickly spread or closed.

Already by the ninth century, Chinese junks were carrying merchants to Indonesia and India. By the 1400s, junks had sailed all the way to East Africa. The Chinese could have easily launched the "Age of Discovery." But in the early 1400s, the Imperial Court of China decided to stop all long-distance voyages. Eventually, the court even prohibited the building of sea crafts. At this time, China worried about land trespassers at its borders. Expeditions at sea took valuable men away from protecting the borders. The junk design was adopted by Western countries in the 1800s and is still used by people in Southeast Asia today.

could set up a padrão on land as a sign of friendship. The ruler granted da Gama's wishes.

After five days in friendly Malindi, the ships started again on their long voyage home. By this time, death and sickness had taken so many crew members, it was impossible to navigate three ships. The men emptied the *São Rafael*'s stores and equipment, and the crew was transferred to the other two ships. After everything had been moved, the crew set the vessel on fire. The crewmen sadly watched the end of the ship that had been their home for a year and a half.

On March 20, the fleet rounded the Cape of Good Hope in a fair wind. The men rejoiced at this point. By now, the survivors had regained their strength and were once again in good health, except Paulo. Paulo had been suffering from a serious lung disease called tuberculosis. Vasco wanted to make it to Portugal before Paulo died. The *São Gabriel* could not get him there fast enough. At the island of São Tiago, Vasco chartered a smaller vessel. He handed over command of the flagship *São Gabriel* to João da Sá. He and his brother then set off for Portugal.

Unfortunately, Vasco's efforts were lost. Paulo's disease rapidly worsened. Vasco refused to let his brother die at sea, where his body would be thrown into the ocean. He landed at the town of Angra, in Terceira of the Azores Islands. He carried Paulo to shore, where he died the next day. Da Gama buried his brother and set sail for Portugal with a heavy heart. Oddly, no one knows for sure what day da Gama finally landed in Lisbon. It was between August 29 and September 1, 1499. As da Gama anchored just below Lisbon, he realized the long, adventurous voyage that had lasted over two years was finally over. He had accomplished the impossible mission.

BACK IN PORTUGAL

When King Manuel heard of da Gama's return, he sent many nobles to bring him to the royal palace. Crowds swarmed in the streets and blocked the palace gates, making it almost impossible for da Gama to pass through. The streets glittered with color. Shawls draped over the balcony railings, and flags fluttered from the rooftops. As da Gama walked by, townspeople threw flowers at his feet. All around, people hailed the hero of Portugal.

EMANVEL I. LVSITANIÆ REX XIV.

When King Manuel I, above, learned that Vasco da Gama had returned to Lisbon, he sent out several noblemen to bring da Gama to the royal palace. After hearing of da Gama's adventures, Manuel knew he must send another fleet to India.

Da Gama's journey of 26 months at sea was the longest voyage and the greatest feat of seamanship at the time.

Surely da Gama did not realize the full impact of his accomplishment. New horizons had been opened. Oceans once unvisited were now charted. Da Gama found a sea road to the Indies—the lands of spices, ivory, gold, and precious stones. He had proved that the waters around India were not separated by land as so many geographers in the fifteenth century believed. The impact was not only one of fabulous trade for Europe, it was also sure to bring trouble and war to the lands of the East. Europeans saw an open door through which to settle, explore, and conquer faraway countries.

The king, too, was anxious to see da Gama. Since the commander had left on a sunny July afternoon, King Manuel had built a high tower at the water's edge. There he sat day after day, wondering if he would ever again see his brave seamen. With wide eyes and a pounding heart, Manuel listened to da Gama's tale of adventure, wonder, and sorrow. Before da Gama had even finished his report, the king had decided he must send another fleet to India. But for now, da Gama rested.

Da Gama was not certain he wanted to continue his career as a sea captain. He was more interested in becoming a wealthy nobleman and land owner. He married a noblewoman, Catherina de Atayde.

This is a garden courtyard at the Convento dos Jeronimos de Belem, near Lisbon. King Manuel I started construction of the convent in 1499 in appreciation of da Gama's successful voyage.

He then asked King Manuel if he could buy his childhood town of Sines. The small town on the sea was neither rich nor fertile. But it had always held his heart. Da Gama believed it was because of his early love of the sea that he had endured the treacherous ocean journey. He had braved the impossible for Portugal's sake. A desolate stretch of land was not too much to ask for. The king was ready to grant his request. But the place belonged to the religious Order of São Thiago, and the order refused to sell the land. Disappointed, da Gama bought a house in Évora. The most the king could do for da Gama was to grant him a pension and give him the title Dom.

In 1500, King Manuel asked Dom Vasco to lead a second expedition to India. After the exhausting two-year voyage, da Gama declined. Instead, Manuel chose Pedro Álvares Cabral. This time, the king sent a fleet of 15 ships carrying hundreds of well-armed men. Unlike da Gama, Cabral was a mild-mannered, even-tempered captain. That did not stop him, however, from visiting punishment on the treacherous town of Mombasa.

The Arabs must have breathed a sigh of disgust when they again saw those square sails puffing toward them, each bearing the hated Christian cross in bright red. But Cabral's attack on the town took the Arabs completely by surprise. The fleet pounded their houses to bits with cannonballs.

Buildings crashed and fell into the narrow streets. Townspeople scaled the rubble and fled into the thick jungle.

Soldiers looted and burned Mombasa. They captured frightened women and tore the jewels right off of them. They carried loads of spoils and riches like they had never seen back to the ships. Cabral certainly taught these Arabs the lesson that da Gama had promised. Like da Gama, Cabral left behind a trail of mistrust and hatred on the coast of Africa. But da Gama was not about to let Cabral finish what he had started. He vowed to one day return, and return he did.

Test Your Knowledge

1 How did da Gama's expedition escape ambush by 70 ships near Calicut?
   a. Da Gama's superior naval skills helped him defeat the enemy.
   b. Da Gama destroyed the lead vessel in the enemy fleet, and the rest scattered.
   c. A strong thunderstorm blew da Gama's ships to safety.
   d. None of the above.

2 What danger faced da Gama's ships in the Arabian Sea?
   a. Dead calm, alternating with strong headwinds
   b. Scurvy
   c. A shortage of food and drinking water
   d. All of the above

3 Why did da Gama burn the *São Rafael*?
   a. It was infested with rats.
   b. So many crew members had died that there were not enough to man the ship.
   c. He feared the ship would fall into Arab hands.
   d. He used the fire as a distraction to escape his enemies.

4　How was da Gama received upon his return
to Portugal?
a. He was hailed as a great hero.
b. He was treated as a pirate.
c. The king refused to see da Gama.
d. None of the above.

5　What did Pedro Álvares Cabral do at
Mombasa?
a. He looted and burned the city.
b. He pounded the houses of Mombasa
to rubble with cannon fire.
c. He captured frightened women and
tore their jewels from them.
d. All of the above.

ANSWERS: 1. c; 2. d; 3. b; 4. a; 5. d

Dom Vasco
da Gama
Sails Again

Vasco da Gama set sail again on February 12, 1502, now Admiral of the Sea of India. This time, his fleet consisted of 20 well-equipped, heavily armed ships. On June 14, the fleet anchored off the port of Sofala, on the East Coast of Africa. Sofala was a poor city but a good exporter of gold, which was mined in the Monomatopa region farther inland. Here, too, was a trade for hippopotamus teeth—harder and whiter than elephant ivory. After a short stop, the fleet continued on its voyage.

The fleet made another brief stop in Mozambique. Da Gama's old enemy, Sultan Khwaza, the sheik of Moçambique, had died since the admiral's last visit. The new ruler was deeply impressed by the white men's courage, intelligence, and weapons. He welcomed the fleet and did all he could to befriend them.

Next, the fleet arrived at the island of Kilwa, which is farther up the African coast in what is now Tanzania. The wealthy city was speckled with fine stone houses. During Cabral's voyage, the ruler of Kilwa had refused to accept Christianity and did not befriend the Portuguese explorer. Da Gama took these actions as hostility. He sent word that he was going to burn the town to the ground if Emir Ibrahim did not pay tribute to King Manuel. Helpless, the emir promised to submit all loyalty to the king of Portugal. As a guarantee that he would pay a tribute to Manuel, Ibrahim sent a citizen of Kilwa to the ship. Da Gama could hold the native prisoner until the payment was made. The prisoner knew that Ibrahim had no intention of paying the tribute and that the Portuguese would probably kill him. So he paid da Gama about $5,000 from his own treasury. Da Gama promptly released the prisoner, never asking who actually paid the tribute.

The crew remained in Kilwa for several weeks, and built a factory for trade on the island. The ships then set sail for Malindi, about 100 miles from Kilwa. Instead of sailing across the Indian Ocean, da Gama stayed near land, past southern Arabia, and down the Indian coast. The fleet anchored again at the Angediva Islands, where they gathered wood and fresh water. They also took the sick crewmen ashore, more than 300 of them. One-third of the crew broke out with scurvy, and many of them died.

From Angediva, the crew sailed for Cannanore, north of Calicut on the Malabar Coast. There, da Gama waited for ships from the ancient city of Mecca. He hoped to attack and loot passing trade ships, taking for the king their cargo of spices and other valuable goods. After several days, an Arab ship, the *Meri*, approached from the west. The vessel belonged to a sailor from Calicut. Besides a cargo of merchandise, the ship carried 380 passengers—men, women, and children. The people were

What Time Is It, Mate?

Portable timepieces, or clocks, had been invented by the end of the 1400s. The very first clocks were made in Germany. But these pieces were large, clumsy, and inaccurate, especially at sea. Da Gama probably did not bring any of these clocks with him on the voyage. Instead, his crewmen measured time in a different way. They used hourglasses filled with sand that ran out every 30 minutes. The best hourglasses came from Venice, Italy. During fierce storms the ships wildly dipped and rocked. Hourglasses often fell to the floor and shattered. Each ship carried an ample supply of hourglasses, in case several would break.

Ship boys were in charge of flipping the hourglass. Each time a glass ran out, the boy rang a bell. The crew used these bells to clock their "watch" time. Sailors had a four-hour watch—eight bells. Today, many ships still ring a bell each half-hour in honor of this tradition.

on their way home to Calicut from a pilgrimage to the holy city of Mecca.

The admiral chased the ship down and quickly overtook it. He ordered the Arabs to hand over the cargo and surrender all their weapons. At first, the Arabs denied having anything valuable on board. In anger, da Gama threw two Arab seamen over the edge of the ship into the ocean, where they drowned. The others quickly confessed to carrying merchandise.

Crew members transferred the cargo to the fleet. But da Gama suspected the Muslims were hiding more goods. He also wondered if they had surrendered all of their weapons. Based on his suspicions, da Gama committed a ferocious act, beyond pirating a peaceful ship. He cold-bloodedly ordered the passengers to be locked in the hold of the *Meri* and the ship set on fire. All on board would be burned to death.

At his command, da Gama's bombardiers set fire to the vessel in several places. The Portuguese fleet pulled away to a safe distance from the flames. When the doomed Arabs smelled the smoke, they broke free from the hold. They dashed about the

An hourglass, an astrolabe, and other instruments were used to navigate during the fifteenth century. Each time an hourglass ran out of sand, a ship boy rang a bell. The crewmen used the bells to clock their time while they were on watch.

deck with buckets of water, dousing the flames. Realizing their fate, the passengers tried to hand over the rest of their concealed weapons in exchange for their lives. Women ran across the deck, holding their children in their arms. They cried and pleaded with the Portuguese to spare them.

Da Gama was not softened. He ordered his men to again set the ship ablaze. From his cabin window, the admiral watched the fire-singed Arabs run about the ship, trying desperately to stomp out the flames. Women and children screamed in fear. Muslims jumped into the sea to escape the flames. The struggle stretched over four days and four nights, with the flames being put out and reignited. Da Gama did not want to waste any more time and was about to give up. Just at this moment, the passengers were betrayed by one of their own people.

One of the Muslims who had jumped off the fiery vessel swam up to da Gama's ship. He bargained with the Portuguese admiral. If da Gama would spare his life, he would swim out and attach a rope to the rudder of the ship with which to start a fire. The passengers would be unable to put it out. Da Gama accepted the offer and spared the man's life.

Without the least bit of pity, da Gama watched the ship burn with everyone on board.

DA GAMA'S REVENGE

After destroying the ship from Mecca, the fleet sailed for Cannanore. On his first voyage, da Gama had sealed a friendship with the rajah there, who was also an enemy of the samorin of Calicut. The rajah welcomed da Gama with a grand ceremony. Da Gama presented him with two hand basins filled with thick coral branches, a very beautiful sight. The two men agreed on a commercial treaty, and da Gama bought spices of all kinds before setting sail again for Calicut.

When da Gama's large fleet appeared before the city, the samorin of Calicut grew nervous and frightened. The ruler at last realized he had made a mistake in becoming da Gama's enemy. He tried to smooth things over and sent his officials out to the ships with an offer of friendship. Da Gama laughed at the samorin's change of heart, and said to the officials that the samorin must banish every Muslim from the city if he wanted peace.

Da Gama wanted to follow up his ultimatum with action. He again acted with cruelty and cold-bloodedness. A number of fishermen had gathered around the boats to sell their catch to the crews. Da Gama commanded his men to capture some of them. The Arabs struggled to get free as da Gama's men dragged them on board.

The captives shuddered in fear. The admiral paced back and forth in front of them. He ordered his men to tie ropes around their necks and hang them from the yardarms. But da Gama did not stop there. At nightfall, he had the dead bodies cut down. Then, he told his men to cut off their heads, feet, and hands. They flung the dismembered bodies over the side of the boat to wash up on shore with the tide. They threw some body parts into a boat and fastened a note to one of the heads. This is the fate of your city, it warned, if you attack us. The boat slowly drifted toward shore.

The next morning, the people of Calicut gathered along the shore, frozen in shock at the ghastly sight. Some Arabs at the water's edge rolled the bodies one by one in search of their loved ones. They searched all day and into the night. Holding flaming torches, they tried to recognize their relatives by their clothing.

Da Gama then sailed with some of his fleet to Cochin to get spices. He left six ships behind to cut off any merchant vessels that tried to enter Calicut. At Cochin, da Gama entered another trade agreement with the city's rajah. On January 3, 1503, an official of Calicut and his son arrived in Cochin. They brought letters from the samorin. The samorin had tried to attack and break the blockade but failed. He asked da Gama to return to Calicut and sign a peace treaty. Da Gama departed at once.

The samorin's invitation was a trap. The Arabs planned to attack and kill the admiral during the night. Da Gama barely escaped with his life. As he had so ruthlessly shown, da Gama was not a man to be toyed with. He released the official, but hung the boy from the sail yardarm. He returned to Cochin to finish his business.

Shortly after, da Gama received a message that the Arabs were putting together a fleet to attack the Portuguese. Da Gama immediately summoned all the ships of his armada to Cochin. On February 10, the armada sailed back to Calicut. Two days later, da Gama crushed the Arab fleet in a short battle.

This tilework shows da Gama aboard his ship near Calicut. On his second voyage to Calicut, da Gama and his men crushed an Arab fleet in a short battle.

With his revenge taken, da Gama ordered the course set for Africa. And on March 5, the fleet began the long journey to Portugal. The second voyage ended in Lisbon on September 1, 1503. Da Gama's expedition had brought many valuable treaties of trade. But it also left a trail of innocent blood and horrible cruelty. Future sailors would reap the consequences of da Gama's steely temper.

Test Your Knowledge

1 What tribute did Emir Ibrahim pay to
da Gama?

   a. One hundred gold bars

   b. His oldest daughter in marriage

   c. Nothing, but da Gama's hostage paid
      about $5,000 from his own treasury

   d. None of the above

2 What became of the Arab ship, the *Meri*?

   a. Da Gama captured it and forced its crew
      to accept Christianity.

   b. Da Gama ordered all its passengers
      into the ship's hold, then had the ship
      burned.

   c. Da Gama's ship sank, so he was forced
      to commandeer the *Meri*.

   d. None of the above.

3 What did da Gama do to the fishermen
of Calicut?

   a. He made them convert to Christianity.

   b. He used them as hostages and demanded
      tribute from the samorin.

   c. He had them hanged, dismembered,
      and thrown into the ocean.

   d. None of the above.

4 Why did da Gama leave six ships at Calicut, while he sailed to Cochin?

 a. To blockade the harbor at Calicut

 b. To negotiate a peace treaty with the samorin

 c. To reclaim the merchandise left by the earlier Portuguese ships

 d. None of the above

5 How did da Gama respond to the Arab fleet?

 a. He sailed back to Portugal.

 b. He crushed the Arab ships in battle.

 c. He entered into a peace treaty with the samorin.

 d. None of the above.

ANSWERS: 1. c; 2. b; 3. c; 4. a; 5. b

Da Gama
as Viceroy

When Vasco da Gama returned from his second voyage, he had King Manuel's highest respect. The king was especially pleased with the tribute from Kilwa. He rewarded da Gama with a pension of 40,000 reis—about $925—a good sum at the time. Da Gama built himself a grand house in

Évora. But he never gave up his dream of owning Sines.

King Manuel was too weak and cowardly to insist that the Order of São Thiago give up its claim. So da Gama once again took matters into his own hands. He moved to Sines and built himself a house. He walked about town in proud strides and acted as if he already owned it. The townspeople hardly minded his arrogance. He was adored by all as the local-born hero of the Portuguese.

Realizing it would be futile to speak to da Gama himself, the order complained to the king. King Manuel ordered da Gama to leave the town within a month, and said he could not return without permission from the order. Although da Gama obeyed, he reminded the king that he had never received the land he was promised in payment for his first voyage.

The courage and skill of da Gama, like that of so many other great men, paved the way for riches and power. But once the door had been opened, the king had little use for him. Lesser men could now travel the sea as he had done. The king could afford to put aside his demands.

Ten years later, Manuel's promise was still unfulfilled. Fed up, da Gama went before the king. He told the king he had waited 10 long years for the land he deserved and said he had no choice but to leave Portugal and offer his services to another country.

King Manuel was startled and worried. But he could hardly forbid da Gama to leave. He told da Gama he could not stand in his way, but he asked him to wait until the end of the year. Da Gama agreed with a bow. Manuel went to work frantically trying to find some land to give the admiral. The king's nephew offered to sell him two towns—Vidigueira and Villa de Frades. In December 1519, da Gama finally received the land promised to him 20 years earlier.

During the years immediately after da Gama's second voyage, Portuguese ships increasingly used the sea route to India. The sailors soon discovered the monsoons blew northeast during one season and southwest during another. They could plan their trips to make good use of these winds. From 1500 to 1504, the Portuguese sailors were mainly merchantmen. Naturally, the ships were armed, but not for conquest. All the king desired was to gain control of India's export trade.

The king, however, could not rely on looting vessels and scattered ports to control the Indian seas. If Portugal was to keep a strong hand on trade, some sort of system for law and order was necessary. In order to establish one, Manuel created a new office—viceroy, or ruler, of India. The main objective of the viceroy was to drive the Muslim traders from the sea. But first, a colony had to be established.

The city of Goa on the central west coast of India seemed the perfect place for a Portuguese colony. The viceroy quickly built up a colonial empire. He brutally wiped out entire Muslim cities and tortured prisoners and survivors. But the colony fell as rapidly as it rose. No one living in Goa cared about the common good. From the governor to the lowest official, each man was in it for himself. Greed ruled rampant and prevented an efficient government. As one Portuguese writer described it: "It was a mixture of perfume and the odor of blood, and of duplicity and cruelty with abject cowardice." [13]

India needed a wise governor, an honest administration. Hopefully, it wasn't too late. This corruption

This is a portrait of Vasco da Gama from a manuscript depicting Portuguese viceroys in India. Da Gama was named viceroy in 1524.

was what Vasco da Gama found as he became viceroy of Portuguese India in 1524.

THE THIRD VOYAGE

The new king—John III—sent Viceroy Vasco da Gama to Goa. The fleet of 14 ships and 3,000 men set sail in April 1524. On this voyage, da Gama took his two sons with him. Dom Estevão went as Captain-Commander of the Sea of India, and Dom Paulo accompanied his father on the flagship. Da Gama was the same harsh, hard-fisted commander who had led the first expedition to India in 1497. Many high-ranking officials died when they were on duty far from home. For this reason, da Gama carried with him three sealed documents that would be opened on his death. The first document named the man who would succeed him as viceroy. The second named the man who would succeed the second viceroy, if he died. And the third named the successor of the second-named viceroy.

After a stop for repairs in Moçambique, the fleet had a terrible turn of luck. Violent storms rose in the ocean, sinking three ships. All crew members perished in the sea. On another ship, the crew mutinied

(continued on page 126)

Navigational Terms From A to Z

Have you ever wanted to talk like a sailor? Here are some terms you can use to sound like a real ship's mate.

Aft—Near the stern, or back end of a ship, for example, "aft of the mast."

Ballast—Heavy material, like sand or stones, placed at the bottom of a ship to give it stability when no cargo is being hauled.

Catheads—Short, horizontal beams on either side of a ship's bow used for raising and stowing the anchor.

Dinghy—A small, open boat with oars, which can be rowed by one sailor.

Figurehead—A carved figure or head at the front of the ship, usually in some way connected to the name of the vessel.

Gig—A lightweight, narrow ship's boat.

Hawse-hole—The hole or pipe in the ship's bow—or on deck—through which the anchor cable runs.

Jacob's ladder—A rope ladder with wooden rungs used for climbing aboard the ship.

Knot—The same as a nautical mile.

Log—Verb: To measure the speed of a vessel from on board. Noun: The ship's diary.

Moonsail—A triangular sail set above the high-set sky sail.

Nautical mile—Equal to 6,076 feet.

Port—The left-hand side of the ship when facing forward.

Quarterdeck—The part of the upper deck "aft of the mainmast."

Rigging—A general term for all the ropes and cables used to work a vessel's spars and sails.

Spars—A general term for masts, booms, yards, and gaffs (the equipment of the sails).

Starboard—The right-hand side of the ship when facing forward.

Trim—To arrange the cargo and gear so a ship will float steady as it should. Also, to set the sails at the most favorable angle to the wind.

Windlass—A revolving machine with a crank used to weigh anchor.

Yard—A rod on the mast to support the sail.

(continued from page 123)

against the captain, murdered him, and sailed away to engage in a career of piracy. Again, scurvy struck the crew, taking many more lives.

When the remaining fleet reached Dabul on the Indian coast on September 8, an underwater earthquake shook the ocean floor. Most of the sailors on board had never experienced such a phenomenon. Suddenly the ships began to pitch and roll. Mariners cried out for God to have mercy, because they thought the ships would capsize. The waters boiled and foamed all around them. The waves tossed the ships so violently that the men were thrown from one end to the other. The quake continued for an hour. All the while, da Gama remained fearless. He called together his crew and assured them, "Friends rejoice and be happy, for even the sea trembles before us." [14]

A few days later, da Gama arrived in Goa. The Portuguese in the colony welcomed the admiral with real joy. They hoped his presence would make life better for them. Da Gama announced himself in an extravagant manner—gold necklaces draped around his neck, dressed in rich clothing, and surrounded by many servants. Many inhabitants of Goa were Arabs. To win their respect, da Gama knew he had to present himself as their native rulers would.

Da Gama used his powers to restore respect and obedience for the government. He learned that some of the king's officers had sold artillery weapons to merchants of the colony. Da Gama immediately ordered these pieces returned, most of which were brought to him at once.

Shortly after assuming his new role, da Gama became ill. The intense heat and overwhelming work made his condition quickly deteriorate. He began having severe neck pains. Eventually, boils broke out at the base of his neck. Doctors tried many remedies, but the sores would not go away. Soon, da Gama could not even turn his head. He took to his bed and issued all orders from there. But his strength continued to fail him, and he realized he was dying.

Da Gama asked to be taken to the house of a friend in Cochin. There, he made his last statements on official matters. A Catholic priest visited his bedside, and da Gama made a confession of his sins and took the sacrament of Holy Communion. He

This statue is on the tomb of Vasco da Gama, who died in 1524. In 1539, his body was returned to Portugal and laid to rest in the ancient church of Our Lady of the Relics in Vidigueira.

then summoned his sons to give his final farewells. At 3:00 in the morning on December 24, 1524, Vasco da Gama died. All of Goa mourned the great admiral's death. Da Gama was buried at a monastery chapel in Cochin until his body could be taken back to Portugal. In 1539, his body was finally returned and laid to rest in the ancient church of Our Lady of the Relics in Vidigueira.

The Indian voyages of da Gama and other Portuguese explorers helped establish Portugal as a world power. Soon, the Portuguese trade empire expanded to China, Japan, the Philippines, and the Spice Islands. Unfortunately, Portugal was too small to control and defend its vast trade network. By the 1700s, the country had lost its position as a world trade power. Before long, the Portuguese outposts were abandoned or destroyed. The jungles grew back over the crumbled buildings, but the memory of these fearless seaman still churns in the coastal currents.

Test Your Knowledge

1 What kind of pension did King Manuel give da Gama?
   a. Ownership of da Gama's hometown of Sines
   b. 40,000 reis (equal to about $925)
   c. Twenty gold bars
   d. None of the above

2 How long did it take da Gama to receive the land granted to him by the king?
   a. 5 years
   b. 15 years
   c. 20 years
   d. None of the above

3 The Portuguese first attempted a permanent colony in India at
   a. Calicut.
   b. Bombay.
   c. Goa.
   d. None of the above.

4 How did da Gama handle the undersea earthquake that shook his fleet?
   a. He never lost his nerve and continued on to India.
   b. He saw it as a sign and returned immediately to Portugal.
   c. He saw it as a sign to convert to the Muslim religion.
   d. None of the above.

In 1524, Vasco da Gama died on

a. Easter Sunday.

b. Christmas Eve.

c. his own birthday.

d. the anniversary of his first voyage.

ANSWERS: 1. b; 2. c; 3. c; 4. a; 5. b

1460 (?)   Vasco da Gama is born in Sines, a small seaside town about 60 miles from Lisbon.

1488   Bartholomew Diaz and his fleet are accidentally swept around the southern tip of Africa. Diaz believes he can find a sea route to India, but his crew forces him to return to Portugal.

1492   Christopher Columbus discovers the Americas.

1497   July 8   Da Gama and the crews of his three vessels set sail from Lisbon in search of a sea route to India.

November 1   The African coast is spotted.

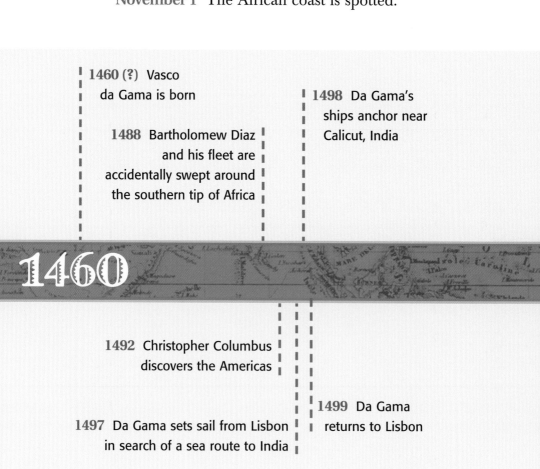

1460 (?) Vasco da Gama is born

1488 Bartholomew Diaz and his fleet are accidentally swept around the southern tip of Africa

1498 Da Gama's ships anchor near Calicut, India

1460

1492 Christopher Columbus discovers the Americas

1499 Da Gama returns to Lisbon

1497 Da Gama sets sail from Lisbon in search of a sea route to India

November 22 Da Gama's fleet sails around the Cape of Good Hope.

1498 March 2 Da Gama's ships anchor near the city of Moçambique, Mozambique.

April 7 The ships near Mombasa, the finest harbor on the East African coast.

April 14 Da Gama's crew drops anchor off Malindi, Kenya, and finds an ally.

May 20 Da Gama's fleet anchors near Calicut, India; the sea route has been charted.

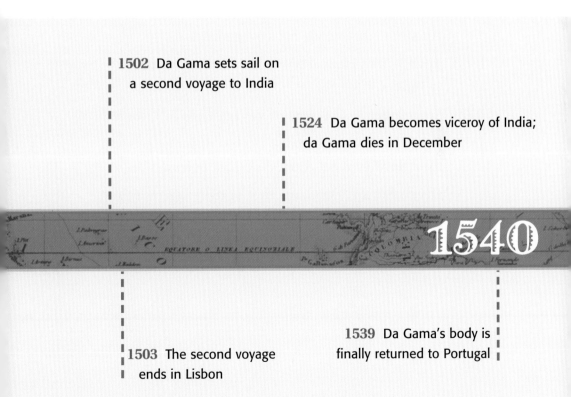

1502 Da Gama sets sail on a second voyage to India

1524 Da Gama becomes viceroy of India; da Gama dies in December

1540

1503 The second voyage ends in Lisbon

1539 Da Gama's body is finally returned to Portugal

May 28 An envoy of Portuguese men goes ashore to meet the samorin of Calicut; the visit turns hostile.

August 29 Da Gama orders his ships to set sail for home; he promises to return and teach the Muslims of Calicut a lesson.

1499   Da Gama's brother, Paulo, becomes sick; da Gama's fleet sails on without him, leaving its commander and his brother in the Azores Islands.

August 29–September 1 Da Gama returns to Lisbon.

1500   King Manuel asks da Gama to lead another expedition to India; da Gama declines, and Pedro Álvares Cabral leads the voyage instead.

1502   **April 1** Da Gama sets sail on a second voyage to India.

1503   **September 1** The second voyage ends in Lisbon.

1524   **April** Da Gama becomes viceroy of India; sets sail for a third voyage; soon, da Gama becomes ill.

December 24 Da Gama dies in the early morning hours.

1539   Da Gama's body is finally returned to Portugal.

Chapter 1
Conquering the Impossible
1. Henry Hart, *Sea Road to the Indies*, New York: The Macmillan Company, 1950, p. 156

Chapter 2
A Brave Seaman
2. Ibid., p. 103.
3. Ibid., p. 107.

Chapter 3
Sailing the Fleet
4. Ibid., p. 118-119.

Chapter 4
Along Africa
5. Ibid., p. 132.

Chapter 5
Trouble in Mozambique
6. Ibid., p. 149.

Chapter 6
India!
7. Kingsley Garland Jayne, *Vasco da Gama and His Successors, 1460–1580.* New York: Barnes & Noble, 1970, p. 52.
8. Ibid., p. 53.
9. Henry Hart, *Sea Road to the Indies*, New York: The Macmillan Company, 1950, p. 177.
10. Ibid., p. 179.
11. Ibid., p. 183.
12. Sanjay Subrahmanyam, *The Career and Legend of Vasco da Gama*, New York: Cambridge University Press, 1997, p. 144.

Chapter 9
Da Gama as Viceroy
13. Henry Hart, *Sea Road to the Indies*, New York: The Macmillan Company, 1950, p. 251.
14. Ibid., p. 254.

Cuyvers, Luc. *Into the Rising Sun: Vasco da Gama and the Search for the Sea Route to the East.* New York: TV Books, 1999.

Gallagher, Jim. *Vasco da Gama and the Portuguese Explorers.* Philadelphia: Chelsea House Publishers, 2000.

Goodman, Joan Elizabeth. *A Long and Uncertain Journey: The 27,000-Mile Voyage of Vasco da Gama.* New York: Mikaya Press, 2001.

Hamilton, Genesta Mary. *In the Wake of Da Gama: The Story of the Portuguese Pioneers in East Africa, 1497–1729.* New York: Skeffington, 1951.

Hart, Henry Hersch. *Sea Road to the Indies: An Account of the Voyages and Exploits of the Portuguese Navigators.* New York: The Macmillan Company, 1950.

Jayne, Kingsley Garland. *Vasco da Gama and His Successors, 1460–1580.* New York: Barnes & Noble, 1970.

Jones, Vincent. *Sail the Indian Sea.* New York: Gordon and Cemonesi, 1978.

Subrahmanyam, Sanjay. *The Career and Legend of Vasco da Gama.* New York: Cambridge University Press, 1997.

Syme, Ronald. *Vasco da Gama: Sailor Toward the Sunrise.* New York: Morrow, 1959.

Books

Boxer, Charles Ralph. *The Portuguese Seaborne Empire, 1415-1825.* New York: Random House, 1969.

Cuyvers, Luc. *Into the Rising Sun: Vasco da Gama and the Search for the Sea Route to the East.* New York: TV Books, 1999.

Gallagher, Jim. *Vasco da Gama and the Portuguese Explorers.* Philadelphia: Chelsea House Publishers, 2000.

Goodman, Joan Elizabeth. *A Long and Uncertain Journey: The 27,000-Mile Voyage of Vasco da Gama.* New York: Mikaya Press, 2001.

Websites

The Sea Route to India and Vasco da Gama
http://www.ucalgary.ca/applied_history/tutor/eurvoya/vasco.html

Vasco da Gama
http://www.cdli.ca/CITE/exgama.htm

Vasco da Gama Collection
http://www.lib.umich.edu/area/sasia/dagama.htm

Rachel A. Koestler-Grack has worked with nonfiction books as an editor and writer since 1999. She lives on a hobby farm near Glencoe, Minnesota. During her career, she has worked extensively on historical topics, including the colonial era, the Civil War era, the Great Depression, and the civil rights movement.

William H. Goetzmann is the Jack S. Blanton, Sr. Chair in History and American Studies at the University of Texas, Austin. Dr. Goetzmann was awarded the Joseph Pulitzer and Francis Parkman Prizes for American History, 1967, for *Exploration and Empire: The Explorer and the Scientist in the Winning of the American West.* In 1999, he was elected a member of the American Philosophical Society, founded by Benjamin Franklin in 1743, to honor achievement in the sciences and humanities.